With the "Eagle Takers"

Hugh, First Viscount Gough

With the "Eagle Takers"

The Peninsular War Experiences of Hugh Gough
with the 87th (The Prince of Wales's Own Irish)
Regiment of Foot

Robert S. Rait

With a Short Historical Record of the 87th (The
Prince of Wales's Own Irish) Regiment of Foot,
During the Napoleonic Period
by Richard Cannon

LEONAUR

With the "Eagle Takers"
The Peninsular War Experiences of Hugh Gough with the 87th (The Prince of
Wales's Own Irish) Regiment of Foot
by Robert S. Rait
With a Short Historical Record of the 87th (The Prince of Wales's Own
Irish) Regiment of Foot, During the Napoleonic Period
by Richard Cannon

FIRST EDITION

Leonaur is an imprint of Oakpast Ltd

Copyright in this form © 2016 Oakpast Ltd

ISBN: 978-1-78282-509-8 (hardcover)
ISBN: 978-1-78282-510-4 (softcover)

http://www.leonaur.com

Publisher's Notes

Contents

'HE HAS HIMSELF AFFORDED THE BRIGHTEST EXAMPLE
OF THE HIGHEST QUALITIES OF THE BRITISH SOLDIER
IN THE ATTAINMENT OF THE GLORIOUS SUCCESSES
WHICH HAVE ATTENDED THE BRITISH ARMY
UNDER HIS COMMAND.'

THE DUKE OF WELLINGTON

Introductory

Readers of *Diana of the Crossways* will remember that the opening scene of that great book is laid in Dublin:

> In the Assembly Rooms of the capital city of the Sister Island there was a public ball, to celebrate the return to Erin of a British hero of Irish blood, after his victorious Indian campaign; a mighty struggle splendidly ended.

Mr. Meredith drew from the life his portrait of that 'fine old warrior, tall, straight, grey-haired, martial in his aspect and decorations,' for he had seen him after his return from the East, old in years, but 'with his uniform and his height and his grey head, like a glorious October day just before the brown leaves fall.' The 'Lord Larrian' of *Diana* was intended to represent Hugh, first Viscount Gough, who had added the Punjab to the Queen's dominions in India. This last achievement was but the culminating point of a life spent in the service of the Empire. The old soldier who unbuckled his sword after his crowning victory of Gujerat, had put on his armour fifty-six years before, and during that long period he had faced his country's enemies in every quarter of the globe. His apprenticeship to the art of war was served in South Africa and the West Indies; he won his early reputation in Wellington's Peninsular army; and he commanded in sixteen separate actions in China and in India. It is the story of this strenuous and devoted life that we propose here to tell.

About the middle of the reign of James I, three brothers, Robert, Francis, and Hugh Gough, made their way from England to Ireland. They were the sons of Hugh Gough, Rector of All Cannings, Wiltshire, and grandsons of John Gough of Stratford, in the same county. All three were graduates of the University of Oxford, and all alike were in holy orders. Their father was also a member of that University; he appears as a clerk of Magdalen College in 1560, and he was Rector of Little Cheverell before being presented to All Cannings in 1593. He married a lady of Devonshire birth, Jane Clifford of Clifford Hall, and, in due course, five of their sons were matriculated in the University.

The brothers, as was not unusual in those days, went up to Oxford in couples; the two eldest, Robert and William, entered Balliol College in 1603, aged nineteen and seventeen respectively; ten years later, another pair, Francis, aged eighteen, and Edward, aged seventeen, became members of St. Edmund Hall; and finally, they were followed by Hugh, who matriculated from New College in 1617. The family included at least two other children, for Hugh is described as the seventh son; but of the others nothing is known. Of the two sons who remained in England, the elder, William, left the university without taking a degree, and became steward to the Earl of Warwick; the younger, Edward, became successively Rector of Great Cheverell, in Wiltshire, and of Over Moigne, in Dorset, besides holding, from 1629, the dignity of a canon of Salisbury.

The founder of the family fortunes in Ireland was the eldest brother, Robert Gough, who became, in 1615, precentor of Limerick Cathedral, and in 1628, Archdeacon of Ardfert. Francis, the most distinguished of the five, left St. Edmund Hall, before taking his B.A. degree, in order to become a clerk of New College, but he had returned to the Hall before proceeding to his Master's degree in 1618. In the same year, he followed his brother to Ireland, and was made Chancellor of Limerick Cathedral. In 1626, he was appointed to the see of Limerick, which he held till 1634, when he died, leaving a family of eight children. The seventh son, Hugh, the bearer of the family name, also found what Anthony Wood describes as 'a just opportunity of going into Ireland,' and in 1626 he succeeded his brother as Chancellor of Limerick, in which cathedral he likewise held a prebend, (from Foster's *Alumni Oxonienses*, Clark's *Register of the University of Oxford*, and Wood's *Athenae Oxonienses*). This Wiltshire family of Goughs, who sided with Church and King in the Civil Wars, must be distinguished from another branch which produced a distinguished Puritan divine and a Cromwellian officer, who was one of the regicides.

There is some dubiety as to whether the family of Gough of Woodsdown, Co. Limerick, to which the subject of this memoir belonged, take their descent from Francis Gough, Bishop of Limerick, or from his brother, Hugh; a persistent family tradition, which can be traced back to the middle of the eighteenth century, asserts that George Gough of Woodsdown, who was born in 1751, was seventh in descent from the bishop.

★★★★★★

The difficulty arises from a question regarding the date of the death of Hugh Gough, the Bishop's younger brother, who, as we have said, succeeded him as Chancellor of Limerick in 1626. A Hugh Gough, Chancellor of Limerick, made his will in 1682, and died in 1684. From this Hugh Gough the first viscount was unquestionably descended, and, if he was the chancellor of 1626, then the family traces its origin not to the Bishop but to his brother. But it seems probable that the testator of 1682 and the chancellor of 1626 are in fact different persons, for, according to Cotton's *Fasti*, (1) in 1662 Hugh Gough, Chancellor of Limerick, petitioned to be excused part of his duties on the ground of 'great age and infirmity,' and (2) in 1670 his office was vacated.

It is not likely that such an office was vacated except by death, and the fact that the testator of 1682 leaves his wife sole executrix seems to suggest that he was a younger man than the chancellor who was very old in 1662. The family tradition is that Hugh Gough, the bishop's brother, died in 1670 at the age of seventy-one (a very old age for those days), and that the Hugh Gough who died in 1684 was his nephew and successor, a son of the bishop. This tradition is supported by a statement made by the Ulster King of Arms in 1816 to the effect that neither of the bishop's brothers, Robert and Hugh, left any issue. If we accept the view here stated, the descent of the family is as follows:—

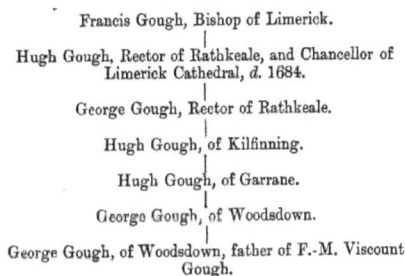

Francis Gough, Bishop of Limerick.
|
Hugh Gough, Rector of Rathkeale, and Chancellor of Limerick Cathedral, *d.* 1684.
|
George Gough, Rector of Rathkeale.
|
Hugh Gough, of Kilfinning.
|
Hugh Gough, of Garrane.
|
George Gough, of Woodsdown.
|
George Gough, of Woodsdown, father of F.-M. Viscount Gough.

★★★★★★

The Goughs had, in the interval, remained faithful to Ireland, and

GEORGE GOUGH, of Woodsdown, co. Limerick (1751–1836), Lt.-Col. City of Limerick Militia, m. Letitia, dau. of Thomas Bunbury, of Lisnevagh.

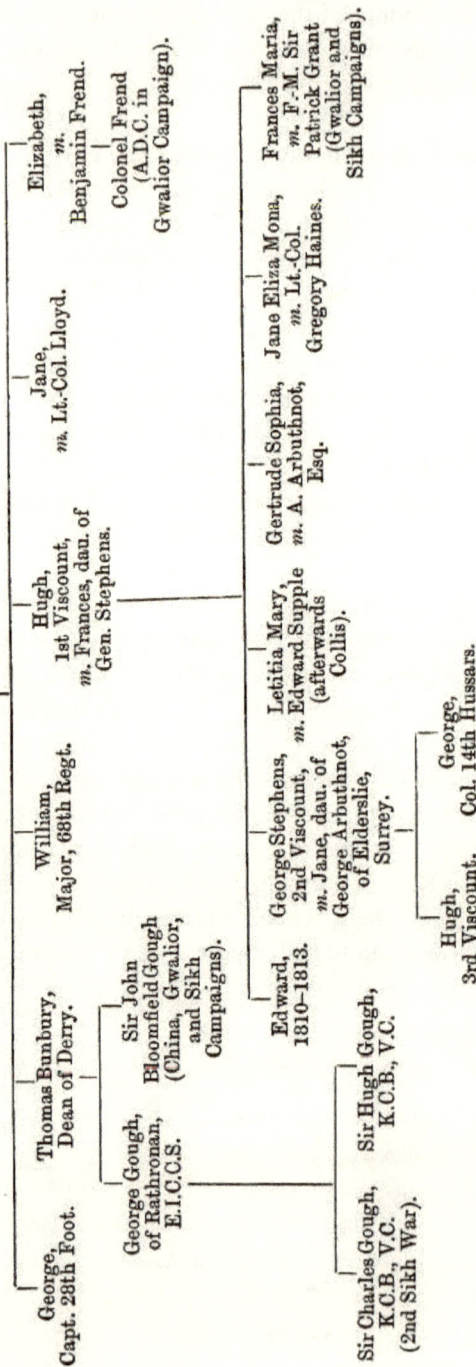

George, Capt. 28th Foot.

Thomas Bunbury, Dean of Derry.

William, Major, 68th Regt.

Hugh, 1st Viscount, m. Frances, dau. of Gen. Stephens.

Jane, m. Lt.-Col. Lloyd.

Elizabeth, m. Benjamin Frend. Colonel Frend (A.D.C. in Gwalior Campaign).

George Gough, of Rathronan, E.I.C.C.S.

Sir John Bloomfield Gough (China, Gwalior, and Sikh Campaigns).

Edward, 1810–1813.

Sir Charles Gough, K.C.B., V.C. (2nd Sikh War).

Sir Hugh Gough, K.C.B., V.C.

George Stephens, 2nd Viscount, m. Jane, dau. of George Arbuthnot, of Elderslie, Surrey.

Letitia Mary, m. Edward Supple (afterwards Collis).

Gertrude Sophia, m. A. Arbuthnot, Esq.

Jane Eliza Mona, m. Lt.-Col. Gregory Haines.

Frances Maria, m. F.-M. Sir Patrick Grant (Gwalior and Sikh Campaigns).

Hugh, 3rd Viscount.

George, Col. 14th Hussars.

had intermarried with families who, like themselves, were of English birth, but resident in Ireland—the Millers of Ballicasey, Co. Clare, and the Wallers of Castle Waller, Co. Tipperary. George Gough of Woodsdown (1751-1836) married, in January, 1775, Letitia Bunbury, the daughter of Thomas Bunbury of Lisnevagh and Moyle, co. Clare, and their descendants added new and greater glories to the traditional distinction which the name of Gough had acquired in the seventeenth century.

George Gough himself had won military laurels in the memorable 'ninety-eight.' He first appears, nine years before his marriage, as cornet 'to that troop, whereof the Earl of Ancrum is captain, in the Fourth Regiment of Horse.' He was, in this respect, following an example set by his father (who had been appointed, in 1756, cornet, and in 1762, captain in a troop of Militia Dragoons). How long he remained under Ancrum is not clear; he makes his next appearance on the stage of history at the outbreak of the troubles in Ireland in 1793. In April of that year he was made Deputy-Governor of the city of Limerick. (The family had been continuously resident near Limerick; e.g. the freedom of Limerick was conferred in 1726 on Hugh Gough of Garrane, the grandfather of the George Gough of whom we are speaking).

A paper of instructions sent to him on his appointment to this office throws some light on the measures taken by the government to suppress the growing discontent. The qualification was a property one; the duties consisted in assisting the mayor in the Militia Ballot, and in aiding him 'to enforce the act against such as are subject to it in respect of serving.' The document closes with this sentence:

> Their (deputy-governor's) office, in short, may be termed Militia Magistrates; within their own jurisdiction therefore, they are as much favoured as any magistrate can be in the execution of his duty, for if any person should be inclined to question their acts, the defence is made as easy as possible to them; it cannot be decided on by any other than a Limerick jury, and treble costs are to be given against the party complaining.

A month later, the deputy-governor was made captain in an infantry regiment of militia; shortly afterwards, he was promoted to a majority, and, in 1797, he became brevet lieutenant-colonel of the Limerick Regiment. He held this office at the date of the rebellion of 1798, and, in July of that year, commanded in a small action, of which a record in his own handwriting has been preserved. A force of about

13

4,000 rebels had gathered in King's County and were laying waste the country in the neighbourhood of Edenderry. Colonel Gough, with 400 of his own Limerick regiment, thirty dragoons, and thirty-five yeomen (cavalry), met them at Johnstown, and completely defeated them, capturing their leaders. His small force lost two men killed and nine wounded. His own horse was hit through the neck, and a shot went through both the cocks of his hat. His conduct received the enthusiastic approbation of one of his commanding officers, and it may be said that his success freed King's County from the insurgents. He says:

This was the second time I saved Edenderry from being burned, as, but that day month before, I got an express sent over to Phillips Town, where I was quartered and commanded the garrison, that a large rebel army had taken possession of Lord Harberton's house, and was encamped on his demesne. I immediately ordered out my division of the Limerick, marched out, and before daylight, Arrived at Lord Harberton's, shot and destroyed all their advanced guard, drove them out of the house, and from their camp, killed 14 of them, and took all their stores, which I next day carted into Edenderry, and shared to all my little party, nineteen stockings a piece. This victory (*i.e.* the success at Johnstown in July) saved Edenderry a second time being burned. I marched back next day, with the blessing of all the inhabitants, who will as long as they live remember Col. Gough and his gallant Garryaon Boys, (an interesting coincidence this song of Garry Owen is associated with his son's Peninsular exploits),— a braver or more loyal, or a more devoted set of fellows to their officers never carried firelocks.

★★★★★★

Note:—The booty on the second occasion included two stands of colours and a telescope, which were retained by the colonel, and '900 pounds in cattle, horses, new linen and spirits,' which he shared with his officers and men; a piece of fine linen which fell to his lot 'I presented,' he says, 'to a very beautiful Quaker lady, at whose house I was that night billeted.'

★★★★★★

Connaught had taken but little part in the rebellion itself, but it was the scene of the abortive French attempt, made after the suppression of the rebels. In August, 1798, a French adventurer, by name

Humbert, landed at Killala, with about a thousand soldiers, trained and disciplined in the Revolutionary wars. It is to the lasting credit of these invaders that they showed to the Irish Protestants and Loyalists the most courteous consideration; and, weary and ill-fed as they were, they fought bravely against overwhelming numbers. They had expected to be received by a united Irish peasantry; but they found no enthusiasm for their cause and were joined by very few recruits. At Castlebar, on August 26, Humbert easily defeated General Lake, whose army, composed of Irish militia, made no effort to stand against the charge of the French. The near approach of Cornwallis, with the royal army, rendered Castlebar unsafe for the invader, and, on September 4, General Humbert commenced a swift march towards Sligo, with the double intention of awaiting reinforcements from France and of gaining Irish recruits in a new district.

The garrison at Sligo consisted of militia troops under Colonel Vereker, whom Colonel Gough had succeeded in the command of the Limerick regiment, which formed part of the Sligo garrison. Vereker seems to have been under the impression that only an advance guard of the French was approaching the town, and, putting himself at the head of 300 men of his old regiment, he marched out to meet them, on the morning of September 5. He had also with him thirty light dragoons and two curricle guns. They met Humbert at Coloney, five miles from Sligo, and maintained a gallant resistance, although the French were many times their number. Finally, they were compelled to abandon their two guns; but Humbert had found their resistance so formidable that, like Vereker, he decided that the enemy must be an advance guard, and he gave up his intention of marching on Sligo (which really lay at his mercy). From Coloney he made his way to Cloone to combine with the rebels at Granard, but he was unable to take all his artillery with him. At Ballinamuck, he found himself surrounded by the armies of Lake and Cornwallis, and, after some resistance, surrendered.

The brevity of the six weeks' campaign in Connaught was largely due to Vereker's defence of Sligo, for if the French had reached the mountains, the resistance would certainly have been prolonged. For his services, Vereker received the thanks of Parliament, and medals were conferred upon the troops engaged. The casualties of the Limerick regiment amounted to thirty-five, and among the wounded was Colonel Gough, who had accompanied his gallant 300 at Coloney. The regiment was disbanded at the Peace of Amiens in 1801, and the historian of Limerick, (*History of the County and City of Limerick*, by the Rev. P. FitzGerald and J. J. McGregor, 1827; Maxwell's *History of the Rebellion of 1798;* Mr. Lecky's *History of Ireland in the Eighteenth Century*), has preserved a record of the scene when the city welcomed back the warriors who had maintained its honour, and when, on the lawn in front of Woodsdown, Colonel Gough bade farewell to his comrades.

The family of Colonel George Gough consisted of four sons and two daughters. The eldest, George, followed his father's footsteps in the Limerick City Militia, in which he received a majority in 1797. It is probable, though there is no evidence on the point, that Major Gough served under his father in the actions we have just described. He afterwards joined the regular forces and served in Egypt and in the Peninsular War as a Captain in the 28th Foot. He died in 1841. Thomas Bunbury Gough, the second brother, entered the Church, and attained the dignity of Dean of Derry. The name of his son, General Sir John Bloomfield Gough, will meet us at a later stage of our narrative; another son, Thomas Bunbury, rose to the rank of Lieutenant-Colonel, and was killed in the attack on the Redan in 1855; and the martial fame of the family has, in modern times, been worthily maintained by several of the dean's grandchildren, among whom the most conspicuous are General Sir Charles Gough and his brother.

General Sir Hugh Gough, who received together the Victoria Cross for valour displayed in the Indian Mutiny; while still more recent campaigns in South Africa and in Somaliland have proved that a later generation is not neglectful of its family traditions. The third son of Colonel George Gough of Woodsdown was Major William Gough, of the 68th Regiment, who served in the Peninsula and in Canada, and who was drowned off Kinsale Head in 1822. Our hero, Hugh Gough, was the fourth son. Of the two daughters, the elder, Jane, married Lieutenant-Colonel Lloyd, who was killed at Bayonne in 1813, and the younger, Elizabeth, married Benjamin Frend, of Boskell, Co. Limerick. Her son, afterwards Colonel Frend, was, like his cousin Sir J. B. Gough, on the staff of his uncle during his Indian campaigns. Mrs. Frend was the favourite sister of the future field-marshal, and to the end of their long lives they entertained for each other the most affectionate regard.

Hugh Gough was born at Woodsdown, on November 3, 1779. Of his childhood, there is nothing to tell, for nothing is known. Family tradition relates that his birth was a disappointment to his parents, who had already three sons, and who had hoped for a daughter; and that the boy was, in consequence, somewhat neglected. He was himself accustomed, in later years, to say that his only education consisted of what he could pick up from listening to the tutor who was teaching his two elder brothers. The real influence of his childhood was, doubtless, the military atmosphere in which he was nurtured, and so powerful was its effect that, at the age of thirteen, he was already wearing the king's uniform. His earliest appointment was in his father's militia corps, whence he passed, almost immediately, to the Hon. Robert Ward's corps, in which he was gazetted Ensign on August 7, 1794. Two months later, he was promoted to a Lieutenancy in the 119th Foot, a regiment raised under Colonel Rochford. He was adjutant of this regiment at the age of fifteen, and there is a tradition that he was reported upon as a specially capable officer.

On June 3, 1795, he was gazetted, by transfer from the 119th Foot, to the 2nd Battalion of the 78th Highlanders, or Ross-shire Buffs (now known as the 2nd Seaforth Highlanders).

Almost seventy years after he had joined the 78th Highlanders, the Lieutenant of 1795, now a field-marshal, had occasion to write to his son-in-law, who had been appointed colonel of the regiment, he said:

> Let me warmly and from the heart congratulate you on your obtaining the colonelcy of my own old (and first corps of the line) the Ross-shire Buffs. I made my debut in them at the Cape when but a boy. . . . How these little incidents recall our memories to days long passed, days of youthful enjoyment, when the participators of them have passed away, and we are standing in hopeful anticipation of rejoining them never to part.—F.-M. Lord Gough to Sir Patrick Grant, November 17, 1863

These sentences, written at a time of deep domestic affliction, constitute the only reference to Lord Gough's connexion with the Seaforths, and it is, therefore, impossible to give any personal details of the boy's share in the actions which resulted in the capture of Cape Town. It may, however, be of some interest to narrate briefly the course of the war, and to indicate the part played by the regiment, (letter quoted in Colonel Hugh Davidson's *History of the 78th Highlanders*).

The first conquest of Cape Colony by Great Britain was an incident in the Revolutionary Wars. In 1794, the French, having defeated the Duke of York near Dunkirk, had Holland in their power, forced the Dutch to renounce their allegiance to the Prince of Orange and to become the allies of the French Republic, and, with the warm support of the democratic party in Holland, founded the Batavian Republic. The Dutch fleet was now at the command of the French Republic, and if the Dutch colonies fell into their hands, the dangers to the British Government would be greatly increased. Two Dutch possessions, in particular, offered a serious menace to Great Britain— the island of Ceylon, from its proximity to our Indian possessions, and the Cape of Good Hope, which was on the road to India. Expeditions were, therefore, sent to take possession of these two colonies in the name of the *stadtholder*, who had taken refuge in England.

In the month of June, 1795, a British force, which included the 2nd Battalion of the 78th Highlanders, arrived off the Cape, and anchored in Simon's Bay. The fleet was under the command of Admiral Elphinstone, and General Craig was in charge of the military forces. Their first step was to ask for an interview, on board ship, with Commissioner Sluysken, the Dutch Governor, and Colonel Gordon, a Scotsman, (Dutch on his mother's side, his father had been in the Dutch service), who was in command of the Dutch forces. This was declined, and the *burghers* immediately took up a position at Muizenburg, about six miles south of Capetown, which commanded the road from Simonstown. A deputation, which included Colonel Mackenzie of the 78th, then landed and proceeded to call upon Sluysken, showing him an order from the Prince of Orange, to receive the troops of his ally, King George.

Such a mandate was unconstitutional, and Sluysken and his council adopted a policy of procrastination. General Craig, in person, explained that the desire of the British was simply to protect the colony, and that there would be no interference with their laws or with any department of their government; but the council answered that they could defend themselves, and would accept of no such help. The British commanders therefore issued a proclamation to the people of the colony, setting forth the dangers of French tyranny and the benefits of His Majesty's protection, (see Theal's *History of South Africa*). This proclamation was regarded as an unfriendly act by the Dutch Council, who forbade the supply of provisions to the fleet and reinforced the garrison at Muizenburg. Gordon was an adherent of the Orange party and was disposed to be friendly if he was satisfied that the British intended only to hold the Colony for the *stadtholder*; but the people were, on the whole, inclined to democratic views, and they welcomed the prospect of hostilities. When it became known in the Colony that the French had respected the separate existence of Holland, and that the States-General had freed the colonists from their allegiance to the *stadtholder*, this feeling increased in intensity.

On July 14, the 78th Regiment (450 strong), accompanied by 350 marines, landed and took possession of Simonstown, and they were soon strengthened by the addition of 800 seamen. General Craig had thus a force of 1,600 men, but he was absolutely devoid of field-guns. The Dutch had less than a thousand men and eleven pieces of artillery, and they occupied a strong position. The British leaders found, in their ships of war, a compensation for their lack of field-guns. On the morning of August 7, the vessels in the bay opened a heavy fire upon the Dutch. The effect was so great that they were driven from their position, but, as the cannonade prevented the near approach of the British infantry, the enemy succeeded in saving some of their guns. Their two cannon they spiked and abandoned.

The Dutch infantry and artillerymen made a stand on a rocky height, out of range of the fire of the ships, and from this they were driven by a charge of the 78th, in which one of their officers (Captain Hercules Scott) and six or seven rank and file were wounded. This was Gough's first experience of hand-to-hand fighting, and possibly the first occasion on which he was under fire. Next morning, there was a further skirmish in which the two Dutch cannon, which had been made fit for use by Craig's orders, were employed against their former owners.

The British now repeated their offers, which were again declined, and they could take no further steps till the arrival of reinforcements. An insignificant action took place on September 1, when the Grenadiers of the 78th silenced an attacking party of the enemy; but there was no decisive step for another fortnight. By the middle of the month, the British forces had been increased to between four and five thousand men. The Dutch were defending Wynberg, on the way to Capetown, and the British attacked on September 14. The enemy were badly led and hopelessly outnumbered, and they made little resistance. Next day, Capetown surrendered, and the colony passed into the hands of the British; to be restored at the Peace of Amiens in 1802, recaptured four years later, and finally to pass under the British crown by the Treaty of Paris.

This was Gough's sole action with the 78th Highlanders. An Irish, not a Scottish, regiment, was his fitting place, and, in December, 1795, he obtained a transfer to the regiment which is most generally associated with his name—the 87th Foot or the Prince of Wales's Irish Regiment. It consisted of one battalion, and had been raised two years previously, largely through the efforts of its commander, Lieutenant-Colonel (afterwards General Sir John) Doyle. It had first seen service in the Duke of York's campaign in the Netherlands, in 1784, and had won a slight distinction in that unlucky enterprise, by repulsing a cavalry attack at Alost. Its next two appearances were not so successful. In 1795 it was stationed at Bergen-op-Zoom, where the desertion of our Dutch allies to the French left it alone in an enemy's country. It was forced to capitulate, and almost the whole regiment became prisoners of war. Its commander did not share its fate, as he was in England, recovering from a wound received at Alost.

By his active interest the empty ranks of the regiment were again filled, and in 1796 it was ordered on an expedition to the North Sea, to aid the troops in the fleet under Lord Duncan; but stress of weather prevented the scheme from being carried into effect. Its destination was now altered, in consequence of an event which startled diplomatic Europe in the summer of 1796. On August 19, Spain, which had long been weary of the struggle with France, and had made peace in the previous year, entered into an offensive alliance with the Republic against Great Britain—an unnatural union which was ere long to meet with fitting punishment. The real importance of Spain, like that of Holland, lay in its naval power, and, to some extent, in its foreign possessions. It was therefore necessary to attack the Spanish, as it had proved necessary to attack the Dutch, colonies, and, in October, 1796, the 87th Regiment sailed for the West Indies.

At what stage Gough joined his new regiment is not clear. A statement of his services, in his own handwriting, dated 1831, mentions that he was present at the capture of the Dutch fleet in Saldanha Bay. This squadron arrived at the Cape in August, 1796, and General Craig, with a force which included the 78th, made a forced march to Saldanha Bay to oppose the landing of any Dutch troops: a march in which considerable suffering was caused by lack of water. There was no fighting, for the Dutch fleet was outnumbered by that under Elphinstone, and surrendered without making any resistance. It will be remembered that the incident was the occasion of an important lawsuit to decide whether the army could claim a share in the spoil, along with the navy. It is not absolutely certain that Gough accompanied the 78th in their march, as he had been gazetted to the 87th nearly a year before; the only clearly ascertained fact is that he witnessed the

HUGH GOUGH

surrender. Shortly afterwards he proceeded to join the 87th.

The first engagement in which Gough served with his new regiment was the attempt on Porto Rico, in the spring of 1797—not an auspicious commencement of a connexion which was destined to bring honour both to the 87th and to himself. In the beginning of April the fleet sailed from Martinique, and, on the 18th day of that month, a landing was effected on the island of Porto Rico. The troops were under the command of Sir Ralph Abercromby, whose intention was to attack the capital—San Juan—a fortified town defended by some thousands of Spaniards and a body of French troops. It was necessary to force a passage over a lagoon which was strongly held by the Spaniards, and the general soon found that the men under his command formed a force quite inadequate for the purpose.

After some days, he determined to abandon the attempt, and ordered the troops to re-embark. He had lost 230 out of his 3,000 men, and was satisfied with the conduct of his army, which he described as 'patient under labour, regular and orderly in their conduct and spirited when an opportunity to show it occurred', (history of the 87th Regiment, Cannon's *Historical Record of the British Army*). Abercromby himself was in bad health and returned to England, and his departure was followed by a complete cessation of hostilities in the West Indies. During this period, the 87th was in garrison at St. Lucia, where it remained till the autumn of 1799. In August of that year, an expedition, commanded by General Trigge and Admiral Lord Henry Seymour, was sent against Dutch Guiana. The force, which included the 87th Foot, proceeded to Surinam, but the Dutch made only a slight resistance, and soon surrendered the town of Paramaribo.

From this date, we are without any definite knowledge of Gough's movements. His regiment remained in the West Indies till the summer of 1804, but the statement of his services, to which we have already referred, shows that he did not accompany it. He speaks of his service in the West Indies as extending over three and a half years, from which we gather that he returned home in 1800; but there is no trace of his doings till June, 1803, when he was promoted to a captaincy. His health suffered considerably from the climate of the West Indies, and he doubtless required some time to recruit. His brother George was engaged in the Egyptian campaign of 1801, and earned a tribute from Sir John Moore for his services at the battle of Alexandria; but we have no evidence of Gough's own presence in any field of action between Surinam and the outbreak of the war in the Peninsula.

The peace which was secured by the Treaty of Amiens, in March, 1802, came to an end in May of the following year. The declaration of war was followed by the assembling of Napoleon's army for the invasion of England, and the threat was answered by the volunteer movement. In addition to nearly 200,000 regulars and militia, a force of 347,000 volunteers was raised in the summer of 1803. Such a force as this required a large amount of training, and we find Captain Gough employed on this task, while his regiment was still in garrison abroad. In June, 1803, he became Superintending Officer of the Army of Defence for the counties of Oxford and Buckingham, and he discharged the same duties in connexion with the Army Reserve.

In a letter written many years afterwards,(Lord Gough to Mr. E. Blakeney, October 27, 1859), he speaks of having gone to the West Indies in the course of this period, and it is possible that he went out in 1804 and returned with his regiment, which landed at Southampton in September of that year. A month later, he accompanied it to Guernsey, and was appointed Brigade-Major to the troops serving in that island, a post which he held till his succession to a majority. This rank he obtained in August, 1805, owing to the 'almost brotherly kindness' of a comrade. Major Blakeney, 'who sold out earlier than he otherwise would have done, in order that I might get his majority,' (Lord Gough to Mr. E. Blakeney, October 27, 1859).

A second battalion of the 87th had been formed in the preceding year, as a part of the reinforcement of the army necessitated by the Napoleonic wars. An Act of Parliament, dated July, 1804, sanctioned the addition of a 2nd battalion to be raised in the comities of Tipperary, Galway, and Clare, and to consist of 600 rank and file, a number which was successively increased to 800 and 1,000, in 1805 and in 1807 respectively. The battalion assembled at Frome, Somerset, in the end of 1804, and in March, 1805, it sailed from Bristol for Ireland. Gough joined this 2nd Battalion at some period in the year 1805; he says, in the statement from which this account is drawn, that he remained at Guernsey till his appointment to his majority in August, and that, thereafter, he served in England, Ireland, and Guernsey.

We are probably right in inferring that, when the 1st Battalion proceeded to Portsmouth in November, 1805, Major Gough did not accompany them, but was attached to the 2nd Battalion which was being trained and recruited in Ireland. It returned to England in October, 1806 (when the 1st Battalion had sailed for South America) and was stationed at Plymouth. Henceforward it is with the 2nd Battalion

BAY
OF
BISCAY
Santander
Gijon
ASTURIAS
GALICIA
C. Finisterre
Minho R.
Oporto
Leon
Burgos
Valladolid
OLD
CASTILE
Salamanca
Segovia
MADRID
BEIRA
Talavera
Toledo
NEW
CASTILE
Peniche
LISBON
Tagus R.
Setubal
Badajoz
ALEMTEJO
ALGARVE
Cordova
Sevilla
Granada
Sierra Nevada
Malaga
Cadiz
Estepona
Gibraltar
Tarifa
Tangier
Ceuta
M E D

MAP

OF

SPAIN & PORTUGAL.

Main Roads. ——— Other Roads. - - - - -

Engl. Miles. 100   0   100

that the name of Gough is connected.

At Plymouth, Major Gough was fortunate enough to meet the lady who was to prove a noble and devoted wife through the joys and sorrows of more than fifty years. Of their first meeting there is a well authenticated story which may bear repetition here. The lady, Miss Frances Maria Stephens, whose father, General Edward Stephens, R.A., was in garrison at Plymouth, was looking forward to a military ball. Before it took place, she told her father that she had seen, in a dream, the man whose wife she was to become, and that he wore the green facings of the uniform of the 87th.

On the night of the ball, she was standing beside her father when Major Gough entered the room, in company with two other officers of the 87th. 'That,' she said, indicating Gough, 'is the man I saw in my dream.' They danced together twice, and the meeting proved the beginning of an acquaintance which quickly ripened into courtship. In April, 1807, the regiment left Plymouth for Guernsey, but, in July, Major Gough returned to claim his bride. Their eldest daughter, Letitia, was born in August of the following year, four months before Major Gough sailed for the Peninsula. Meanwhile, the newly-raised battalion had been undergoing a course of training under Lieutenant-Colonel Doyle and Major Gough. It was carefully inspected in the month of June, 1807, and reported fit for active service, to which Napoleon's interference in the affairs of Spain promised soon to call it.

In June, 1808, the 87th left Guernsey, and, after a period of training at Danbury Camp, embarked at Ramsgate. The Colonel-in-Chief at this time was General Sir John Doyle, whose nephew, Lieutenant-Colonel Charles Doyle, had been actually in command of the battalion, but was now employed as a Military Commissioner in Spain. The command of the regiment, therefore, devolved upon Major Gough, whose fortunes in the Peninsula we proceed to follow. This can be done in considerably greater detail than has been possible up to the present point, both because the sources of information become more abundant, and because the personal share of Major Gough in the deeds of his regiment now begins to be important.

1: Talavera and Barrosa

The 'Continental System' by which Napoleon attempted to crush the commercial power of Great Britain was directly responsible for his first interference in the affairs of the Peninsula, for it was the hesitation of the Prince Regent to carry out the Berlin Decrees that brought about the famous decision that 'The House of Braganza has ceased to reign,' and the consequent occupation of Lisbon by the French under Junot. Within a year the Spanish House of Bourbon had also been deposed, and the Government of George III found that they were now in a position to resist Napoleon's schemes in Portugal, and in Europe generally, with the co-operation of their old enemies, the Spanish nation. With the initial campaign of 1808 we are not in any way concerned. It resulted in the evacuation of Portugal by Junot and in the supersession of Sir Hew Dalrymple and Sir Arthur Wellesley, in view of the popular indignation caused by the Convention of Cintra.

While Wellesley was in England, defending his conduct, and Napoleon was leading the '*Grande Armée*' to Madrid to re-establish his amiable but incompetent brother, Joseph, on the Spanish throne. Sir John Moore was in command of the British Army in Portugal. He had succeeded in making good his retreat into Galicia, and in enticing Napoleon to follow him, when the revolt of Austria recalled the emperor from the Peninsula, leaving Marshal Soult to prevent, if he could, the escape of the British forces by sea from Corunna. The victory of Corunna secured Moore's main object—the loss of some months to the French in their conquest of Spain; he had wasted their time in a fruitless pursuit, and his own army embarked in safety.

The death of Moore left Sir Arthur Wellesley. whose reputation had emerged unsullied from the investigation, the only possible British commander. The ministry of the Duke of Portland numbered among its members Canning as Foreign Secretary, and Castlereagh as Secretary of State for War. Divergent as were the characters and ultimately the aims of these two statesmen, they were united in a common attachment to Wellesley, and in a common belief in his powers, and it should be recorded to the credit of Castlereagh that, through good and evil report, he continued to give a loyal support to his general.

The Battle of Corunna was fought on the 16th of January, 1809; and about two months later Wellesley arrived in Lisbon and advanced against Soult in the district of the Douro. Among the 30,000 troops which were soon at Wellesley's disposal for the summer campaign was the 2nd Battalion of the 87th, under the command of Major Gough, acting for Lieut.-Colonel Charles Doyle, whose services were required elsewhere. A few months before embarking, when he took sole command of the battalion at Danbury, he had been compelled to employ strong measures to improve its discipline.

This task had been largely accomplished when the battalion sailed in December, 1808, forming part of the force which Sherbrooke unsuccessfully attempted to land at Cadiz in February, and, owing to the opposition of the Spaniards, had to take back to Lisbon, where it was disembarked in March. The battalion was attached to Tilson's brigade and it took part in Wellesley's first operations, which, by the passage of the Douro and the capture of Oporto (May 12, 1809, resulted in the expulsion of Soult from Portugal, For this period of the campaign none of Gough's letters to his wife have been preserved, but there is an extant letter addressed to his father from Guards on the 23rd of June, 1809. It gives an account of the tiresome and difficult march in which the battalion was engaged. Unfortunately, it is in a very bad state of preservation, and there are considerable gaps which can only be filled by conjecture:—

Bishop's Palace, Guarda; June 23rd, 1809.

My Dear Father,—As I am persuaded you feel much interested in the movements of the 87th Rt, I shall detail them to you, as far as my recollection will carry me, from our leaving Quimbra. In my letter of the 4th May from that town, I believe I mentioned to you, that the 5th Bat of the 60th, the 87th, and 88th Regts,, under Major General Tilson, and a squadron of the 14th and some German Lt. Dragoons, under Colonel Talbot, were destined to Act with the Portuguese Army, the whole under Genl. Beresford. To our brigade was attached a regt. of Portuguese grenadiers, and a regt. of native cavalry was placed under Colonel Talbot. The Intention was to have forced the passage

31

of the Douro at Lamego, and attack a French division of 4,000 men that had occupied the strong position of Amaranthe under Genls. Labord and L'Ouisson (Loison), while the army, under Sir Arthur, Invaded the town of Oporto. We marched on the 6th from Quimbra, and crossed the Douro without the (slightest trouble) on the 12th, although the enemy occupied the hills, which completely commanded the passage.

The brigade halted that night at Rigoa (Pero de Ragoa). (The depot for all the wine made on the north side of the Douro—the best in Portugal, and where it is shipped for Oporto, 10 leagues distant.) The next morning at daylight we marched for Amaranthe. Within a league of this once beautiful town, we found the cavalry and some Portuguese regts. had halted for us. As it was reported, the enemy were determined to maintain the position, the 87th were honoured in being ordered to lead the attack on the town and bridge. As we advanced, we had to pass through various villages, which were invariably found smoking in their ruins. This so enraged the men that it was with difficulty they could be kept back. I never witnessed so much enthusiasm as was shewn by the men.

The advance, therefore, was a perfect trot. But the British were destined to be disappointed, as on our arrival we found the enemy had fled, and this once beautiful town one undistinguished ruin. I never was a witness to such a scene of misery and horror as here presented itself. Every house and public building of every description with the exception of a monastery, that covered the passage of the bridge, a chapel and about 5 detached houses, were burnt to the ground, with hundreds of its late inhabitants lying dead in the streets. The reason of the hasty retreat of the French that morning was the Battle of Oporto—if battle it could be called, which took place the preceding day. Otherwise, they might have made a very desperate stand, as the position was wonderfully strong.

We left this scene of misery on the 15th, having the evening before received. Orders to proceed to Chaves by forced marches. Within a league of the town we had to ford the Tarmagar (Tamega), a small river in dry weather. It was the turn of the 87th, unfortunately, to be the rear regt. of the column this day. The 60th crossed with the loss of one man. The 88th took so long a time to ford it, that when the 87th Grenadiers came to cross, the river presented a most formidable appearance. In short, the river rose so fast, from the dreadful rain of the preceding evening, and that morning, that the men were above their middles in a flooded mountain river, in which the current was wonderfully rapid.

One officer and 14 privates were carried down by the stream, but were providentially saved by the exertions of the mounted officers. Two companies were unable to pass. Here the misfortunes of the brigade commenced. The whole of the men's bread, which was made of Indian corn, got wet and was destroyed. Several thousand rounds of ammunition were rendered unserviceable, without a possibility of replacing it. A number of firelocks, caps and shoes were lost. The business of crossing the river took the brigade 4 hours. The evening set in with a most dreadful fall of rain, which continued all night and the (next three) days and nights . . . (On the first day we) had three leagues, upwards of fourteen miles, to march, although we left Amaranthe at 4 in the morning.

Our road lay over almost impassable mountains, made more so by the dreadful rain that swelled the mountain rivulets into rivers. The night turned out as dark as it was possible. The men were obliged to move in Indian files, and actually grope their way—no torches being provided, and the rain preventing lighted straw from being of service. As there was no road, many men lost the column, several fell into pits, excavated by the falling of the waters, numbers lay down in the river from fatigue and hunger, and the greater part of the brigade lost their shoes. At length, after grouping in the dark, totally unconscious whether we were right or wrong, from 8 until 9 o'clock, the brigade arrived at a straggling village.

Some got shelter, others did not. I was fortunate in meeting an inhabitant with a light, and getting shelter for all of the regt. that were able to come up. At 5 next morning we pursued our march, but without provisions, as we only n`eed, two days' bread, and one day's meat, the evening before we left Amaranthe, and the bread was either destroyed in the river, or by the rain. This day proved as wet as the two preceding. At 10 o'clock at night we reached a wretched little village on the mountains (quite) incapable of housing a company. We pursued our melancholy march at 5 o'clock next morning, the men nearly fainting with hunger. We, however, most fortunately at 12 that day fell in with some cars of bread belonging to a Portuguese division.

Genl. Tilson immediately pressed it for the men, which, with some wine, enabled us to proceed, and we that night at 12 o'clock got to Chaves, the most northern frontier town in Portugal, after a forced march of three days—with only twelve hours' halt—over almost impassable mountains, the men without a shoe to their feet, and some hundreds of the brigade fallen out from fatigue and hunger. The officers commanding regts. were ordered to assemble next morning at 10 o'clock at Genl. Beresford's, when we were told that the enemy had fled from Oporto, and then were within some leagues of us, that it would be necessary for the brigade to march at 1 o'clock. We, however, did not march until three—and even then the men's meat was uncooked from the lateness of the issue, and not a single pair of shoes could be got in town.

We slept on the Spanish mountains that night. The next day, when within two miles of the village of Ginco in Spain, the advance came up with a party of the enemy. We were again ordered to lead the Attack, and although the men were but the minute before apparently incapable of marching a league, this news had the power of reanimating them, and we past through the Portuguese as if the men had not gone a mile. The British were here again destined to be disappointed, as the (enemy consisted) mostly of cavalry and fresh. They retreated much faster than we could advance. Their exact amount could not be ascertained, but Talbot, who was within a few hundred yards of them, took them to be about 400.

They joined Soult a league and a half to our left, and the whole proceeded in their retreat, amounting to 9,000, out of 22,000 he brought into Portugal but a short time before. Here the pursuit was given up as fruitless, we having taken 45 poor wretches. The brigade was nearly annihilated (by the fatigues) on the road—and I was by far the most fortunate regt. I had (still . . . men. The 88th), out of 700 they joined us with, did not bring 150 into . . . part of the officers and almost all the men I brought up, had not a (shoe to) their feet, which were actually cut to the bone. We halted a day and returned by Chaves to Lumago, and from thence here. All our sick, with very few exceptions, we picked up on the road. But we have since suffered much from sickness.

Nine officers and 47 men have been attacked by some fever in Lumago, and while in this town several have died from the fatigue. I have been unfortunate, as I was attacked by a most violent fever on my arrival here, which, with two slight relapses, (kept me idle for a) month. (Out of this) . . . time I kept my bed for a fortnight. I am, however, so wonderfully recovered that I set off in two days to join the regt. at Castile Branco, 14 leagues distant, to which they marched on the 12th, leaving me in bed. I have now, my dear father, given you a long, and I apprehend you will consider, a very tedious detail of the operations of the British Brigade.

But as there has been some misunderstanding between our Genl. Tilson and the senior officer, Beresford, who, unfortunately, had to report on the conduct of the brigade, although he never saw them—which report I apprehend from Genl. Tilson resigning and going home to England, has not been favourable, and may come to a public investigation, which I ardently hope may be the case for Tilson's sake—I am anxious to put you in possession of all our movements. I had flattered myself the name of the 87th Regt. would have appeared in the papers. But the occurrences of the few last weeks have fully proved to me that war is but a lottery, and those who least deserve may be those who get most credit. I have not had a line since the 9th April.

Believe me. My Dear Father,
Ever Yours Affectionately,

H. Gough.

P.S. I understand General Tilson's parting orders to the brigade are very flattering. I shall send a copy to Frances when I get to Castle Branco.

In June, the army was formed into divisions, and the battalion was given a place in the 2nd Brigade of the Third Division, under Donkin, who was appointed to succeed Tilson, now in command of a brigade of Hill's division. Under Donkin's leadership, the 87th accompanied Wellesley's advance into Spain, and took a distinguished part in the campaign of Talavera. The British Army found their task more difficult on Spanish than on Portuguese soil, and Wellesley had to secure the co-operation of the Spanish general Cuesta, so it was not till the end of July that he found himself face to face with Marshal Victor near Talavera.

Into the details of the battle it would be wandering too far from our subject to enter, nor is there any need to repeat the oft-told tale. The Battle of Talavera was fought on the 28th of July. On the preceding evening, an attack was made on the Casa de Salinas, a hill on the left of the British position. It was, in Napier's opinion, the key to the position, and it was held by Donkin's Brigade. The sudden assault of Ruffin and Villatte took the British by surprise, and the French gained for a time the summit of the hill. In the severe fighting which followed, Donkin's Brigade were, with the help of reinforcements, ultimately able to maintain their ground, but not without considerable loss. In the action of the following day, Gough was severely wounded by a cannon shot on his right side, accompanied with fracture of one of the lower ribs. Twenty-seven other officers of the battalion were also wounded, and so great were the losses in rank and file, that it was sent into garrison when Wellesley retreated into Portugal.

Donkin wrote to Gough on the 15th of September:

Reduced as the Battalion now is chiefly by its losses on that occasion (Talavera), it is evidently no longer a corps effective for field operations, and on this occasion you are going into garrison. The cause, therefore, of your retiring from the field carries with it its consolation, and I trust that the reinforcements you seem to expect from England will enable you soon to join us again.

Donkin took the opportunity of conferring the highest praise upon Gough and his men, and two months later, when leaving for England, he added to his words of farewell—

Permit me on this occasion, too, to repeat the assurance of the high sense I entertain of your personal exertions and gallantry at Talavera, until the moment when I was deprived of your assistance by your being wounded and taken off the field.

The battalion was sent to Lisbon, where it remained in garrison while the commander-in-chief (now Viscount Wellington of Talavera) was preparing the lines of Torres Vedras for the ensuing campaign against Massena. Gough was with his regiment as late as November 26, when he wrote to his wife from Lisbon; but his wound was giving

BATTLE OF FUENGIROLA, OCTOBER 15, 1810

him considerable trouble, and he was allowed a short visit to England, in which to recruit. The date of this visit is uncertain. There is a pause in the correspondence from November to June, and during part of this time he must have been at home. In February, his regiment was transferred from Lisbon to Cadiz, and his next letter to Mrs. Gough is dated from the Isla de Leon on June 3. At Cadiz it was not purely garrison work that occupied the attention of the troops. The progress of the French operations in Andalusia, which Soult had invaded in the beginning of 1810, led to a blockade of Cadiz by Marshal Victor, which was destined to continue until the withdrawal of Soult's army from Andalusia in the autumn of 1812. By the end of the month of February, 1810, the French had obtained complete possession of Andalusia, with the exceptions of Gibraltar and Cadiz, and it was more by good fortune than by good management that Cadiz did not fall into the hands of Victor in the course of his first attempt. Cadiz was saved by the British command of the sea, which allowed Wellington to throw into the beleaguered town a fresh garrison, including the 2nd Battalion of the 87th.

When General William Stewart arrived at Cadiz in February, 1810, the garrison of Cadiz consisted of some 3,000 British troops, and about 14,000 Spaniards, along with a number of Portuguese. Stewart's most important service was the recovery of a fort called the Matagorda which had been unwisely abandoned. In the end of March a new commander arrived—General Graham (afterwards Lord Lynedoch). He had entered the army late in life, and had but little military experience. It is interesting to recall the fact that, in boyhood, he had possessed (in common with the father of Sir Charles Napier) no less distinguished a tutor than David Hume. When Graham took charge, he found that the defences were in a most miserable condition, and their improvement required a considerable addition to his available forces.

Reinforcements arrived, and Graham, in spite of some difficulties with the Spaniards, carried out an important scheme of fortification, interrupted by violent assaults upon Matagorda. In July, the numbers of the garrison were still further increased to 30,000 allied troops. Thus the summer and autumn passed, the French unable to capture the place, but maintaining a strict blockade and rendering it impossible for the garrison at Cadiz to be transferred to another part of Andalusia. The loss of Cadiz would have been second in importance only to that of Gibraltar, and would have made it impossible for the allies to continue to hold any part of the south-west of Spain. No incident of the blockade calls for our attention until we reach the memorable Battle of Barrosa.

From the date of the Battle of Barrosa (March 5, 1811) onwards, almost to the close of the War, our information regarding Gough's personal share in the campaigns becomes much more complete, as the letters of this period have been preserved along with various documents, relating to the military operations in which the battalion was engaged. We left the 87th at Cadiz, forced to remain inactive, while the fate of Southern Europe was depending upon the success of Wellington's great defence of the lines of Torres Vedras. Occasional attempts upon French outposts at Moguer and Huelva varied the monotony of garrison life, but of these Gough's correspondence says nothing, and the efforts to reduce these defences of the main French position at Seville were unavailing. In September, 1810, a meeting of the Spanish Cortes (the first since 1808) was held at Cadiz, and it exercised considerable influence upon the course of the war.

One of the fashionable constitutions of the time was drawn up, based upon a democratic principle which would have proved impossible of realization in any European country, and which was peculiarly unsuited to the traditions and the circumstances of Spain. The resistance to Napoleon had not been merely the natural opposition to a gratuitous war of conquest, nor was it merely against the pride of an ancient race, with traditions of imperial sway, that the French had offended. The shock of the French Revolution had come with special force upon a haughty nobility, accustomed to receive a deference which seemed to be founded upon the immutable laws of nature; upon a clergy whose influence had remained undisturbed by the religious revolution of the sixteenth century; and upon a people which had been wont to render unquestioning obedience to its leaders.

The principles of the pre-Revolution philosophers had not spread from France into Spain, as they had spread into England and America. The rise of a military despotism, and the overthrow of the ancient constitutions of Europe had increased the horror with which the tenets of democracy were regarded by the larger portion of the Spanish people, and the war was waged against the Revolution, and all that the Revolution stood for, as much as against the emperor and Joseph Bonaparte. This national feeling, which had given point to the famous remark of Sheridan that Napoleon had 'yet to learn what it is to combat a nation animated by one spirit against him,' was outraged by a Cortes which claimed for itself the title of Majesty, and allowed

Campaign of
BARROSA
Feb. – March, 1811
Scale, 1:1,000,000
English Miles

Graham's route

ATLANTIC OCEAN

Cadiz
Sta. Maria
Rota
Puerto
To Seville
Puerto Real
To Fonda
Medina Sidonia
CRUZ AGNE
Casas Viejas
Plain of La Janda
To Ronda
To Cordova
San Roque
Gibraltar
Str. of Gibraltar
Tarifa
Feb. 24 - 25
Facinas
Algeciras
Vejer
R. Barbate
C. Trafalgar
Conil
Torre Barrosa
Casas de las Gazolias
Torre Bermeja
San Fernando
Island of Leon
Chiclana

to the Regents for the ancient monarchy only that of Highness. With an amount of folly for which it is difficult to make due allowance, the Cortes proceeded to outline a number of proposals which could not but divide the national resistance still further, and along more definite lines.

An attack upon the privileges of noble blood alienated the aristocracy; a suggested interference with the powers and functions of the Inquisition made the clergy doubt if things would be worse under the rule of the French. The Spanish colonies, which had not been backward in contributing aid to the mother-country, were treated with a contempt worthy of the despotic rule of Philip II, and the Cortes entered upon a course which finally provoked the revolt of the colonies, and the serious complications which that rebellion involved. From the month of September, 1810, Spanish feeling ceased to be unanimous, and the sympathy between the British and the Spanish peoples, of which this is the first instance in history, now reached its period of decline, as the main aims and objects of the allies began to diverge.

The immediate effect of the meeting of the Cortes was a change in the personnel of the Spanish Generals. Andalusia was placed under the charge of Manuel La Peña, and he was also entrusted with the command of the Spanish forces which guarded the Isla de Leon. It had been intended that La Romana should join La Peña at Cadiz, but at the instance of Wellington, he was retained in his command in the army which was facing Massena, and General Graham was left to concert with La Peña a scheme of defence against the renewed attack upon Cadiz, for which the enemy had been busily preparing. To appreciate the situation which led up to the Battle of Barrosa, it will be necessary to give some account of the fortifications of Cadiz, and of its topography, as far as concerns our story.

Cadiz is situated upon a small rocky peninsula at the end of a narrow isthmus, about five miles long, known as the Isthmus of Cadiz. This isthmus projects from a flat triangular marsh, broken by a central ridge, on which stands the town of Isla. Beyond this marsh (the famous Isla de Leon) is the Channel of Santi Petri, extending round two sides of the triangle formed by the Isla, and separating it from the mainland. The French had invested Cadiz from the mainland, by means of a chain of forts, stretching from the mouth of the River Guadalquivir, some twenty miles north of Cadiz, to a point about five miles south of the Santi Petri. The main positions in this line were Puerto Santa Maria, at the mouth of the Guadelete; Puerto Real, at

43

the root of a tongue of land projecting, for a distance of four miles, towards the Isthmus of Cadiz; and Chiclana, a strong position almost opposite the southern mouth of the Santi Petri channel.

The tongue of land projecting from Puerto Real is intersected by a canal known as the Trocadero; and at its southern extremities, facing the Isthmus, were the fort of Matagorda, on the north of the canal, and the fortified village of Trocadero on the south. To the north of Puerto Real, the French held the coast towns of Rota and San Lucar. The defences of Cadiz consisted, in the last resort, of the communication between the town and the Isthmus, which would probably have rendered the place really impregnable had any of the French attacks penetrated so far. The Isthmus itself was divided almost at right angles, by a creek called the Cortadura, at the top of which was an unfurnished fort called Fernando.

A battery at Puntales, on the Isthmus and opposite to the village of Trocadero, commanded the approach to the north end of the Santi Petri. Close to the junction of the Isthmus of Cadiz with the Isla de Leon, was the Torre Gordo, which offered another point of vantage for the defence. Finally, the Spaniards held the Santi Petri Channel, by means of an island at each end. The only communication between the Isla de Leon and the mainland was by a bridge at Zuazo, which crossed the Santi Petri at a point near its centre, whence a road led directly to the town of Isla and thence to Cadiz. This bridge had been broken down, and each side had protected itself by a battery on its own side of the channel. The Spanish command of the Santi Petri was, however, more apparent than real, because the coast line consisted, on the mainland, of a marsh, from one to three miles broad, intersected by navigable channels and creeks of considerable size.

On the 31st of October, 1810, the French succeeded, by an ingenious stratagem, in adding considerably to their numbers and resources. Part of their available force was at San Lucar, watched by a hostile fleet, in spite of which thirty pinnaces and gunboats managed to escape, and reached the town of Rota, whence they made their way to Puerto Santa Maria. So strong was the battery at Puntales that they did not risk an attempt to get into the Trocadero canal by sea, but conveyed their ships on rollers overland. This accession to the strength of the enemy at the Trocadero batteries was intended to threaten Puntales, and ultimately to open the Santi Petri to the French fleet, thus giving them the command of the Isla de Leon, and reducing the allied forces in Cadiz to their last line of defence.

BATTLE OF BARROSA

Reinforcements were immediately sent from Gibraltar, and Graham devised a scheme for strengthening the defences, which the Spaniards were too busy to carry out. Fortunately, the attack which Soult is supposed to have meditated upon the fort of Puntales and the defence of the Cortadura, was prevented by the course of events in another portion of the area of warfare. The strategy of Wellington at Torres Vedras led Napoleon to send instructions to Soult to go to the assistance of Massena, and in the end of December he left Cadiz to reduce the fortresses of Olivenza and Badajos, as a preliminary to carrying out the emperor's orders. The French Army at Cadiz were left under the command of Marshal Victor, and General Graham felt himself strong enough to make an effort to raise the siege.

Graham's plan was to combine with the troops stationed at Tarifa, under Lieut.-Col. Brown, and with a body of Spaniards under Beguines, in an attempt upon the rear of the French lines; but as he was prevented, by stress of weather, from either carrying out his own part of the movement, or communicating with the other commanders, the scheme had meanwhile to be abandoned. The result was considerable delay in making the great effort, and it was not till February 22, that Graham actually set sail from Cadiz, and landed at Algesiras, ready to resume his operations for a rear attack upon the enemy who were threatening Cadiz. Gough says:

On the 24th we marched to Tarifa, where we were joined by six or eight thousand Spaniards. We had about 4,000 men. . . . The object of the expedition I hardly know.—Letter of March 6, 1811.

The British troops under Graham's command, when the army left Tarifa, consisted of a detachment, numbering about two hundred, of the 2nd German Hussars under Major Busch; about three hundred and fifty Royal Artillery and Royal Artillery drivers under Major Duncan; of two brigades, commanded respectively, by Brigadier-General Dilkes and Colonel Wheatley; and of two detached light battalions under Lieut.-Col. Brown, and Lieut.-Col. Barnard. The first of the two brigades included the 2nd Battalions of the 1st and 3rd Guards, and of the Coldstream Guards, with a detachment of the 2nd Battalion of the 95th; the second, the 1st Battalion of the 28th and the 2nd Battalions of the 67th and 87th; Brown had the flank companies of the 1st Battalions of the 9th and 28th Foot; and of the 2nd Battalions of the 82nd and 47th Foot; while Barnard commanded a detachment of the 3rd Battalion of the 95th Foot, and a company of the Royal Staff Corps. Wheatley's division also contained the flank companies of the 20th Portuguese.

Of the Spanish forces, a portion had been left under General Zayas, to protect the Isla de Leon, and to construct a bridge over the Santi Petri, near the castle of the same name. The 7,000 to whom Gough refers as joining Graham at Tarifa, were under the direct command of La Peña, who asserted his claim to take charge of the whole operation. Graham gracefully yielded this point, and the march was commenced, towards Chiclana, where about 11,000 French awaited them. On the 2nd of March, La Peña's vanguard took the fort of Casa Vieja. On the 4th, the army marched out of the Casa. The story of how the British force, designed to attack the French rear, were themselves attacked in rear, how they countermarched, and how they defeated the enemy is familiar to all who are acquainted with the campaigns in the Peninsula, but Major Gough's correspondence throws some fresh light on the narrative. The events which led up to the Battle of Barrosa may best be described in the words of Graham's dispatch:—

> After a night's march of sixteen hours, we arrived, on the morning of the 5th, on the low ridge of Barrosa, about four miles to the Southward of the Santi Petri River. This height extends inland about a mile and a half, continuing on the North the extensive heathy plain of Chiclana. A great Pine Forest skirts the plain, and circles round the height at some distance, terminating down to Santi Petri; the intermediate space between the north side of the height and the forest being uneven and broken.
>
> A well-conducted and successful attack on the rear of the Enemy's lines near Santi Petri, by the vanguard of the Spanish Army under Brigadier-General Lardizabal, having opened the communication with the Isla de Leon, I received General La Peña's directions to move down from the position of Barosa to that of the Torre Bermeja, about halfway to the Santi Petri river, in order to secure the communication across the river, over which a bridge had been lately established. This latter position occupies a narrow woody ridge, the right on the sea-cliff, the left falling down to the Almanza Creek on the edge of the marsh. A sandy beach gives an easy communication between the western points of these two positions.

On receiving La Peña's orders,. Graham sent out cavalry patrols to

BATTLE OF BARROSA

discover if the enemy were moving from their lines at Chiclana. They failed to report any such movement, and Graham, about the hour of noon, set out through the pinewood in front of the height of Barrosa, to effect a junction with La Peña at Bermeja. The idea of a junction at Bermeja did not meet with Graham's approval. He mentions in his dispatch that he considered Barrosa to be the key to the position of Santi Petri, and that an attack by the French upon the Spaniards at Bermeja would have exposed their flank to the British forces on Barrosa. He therefore left a rearguard on the top of the hill, under Brown.

The march to Bermeja was only two miles, but before it was completed, Graham was informed that the enemy, whom his patrols had not succeeded in locating, had emerged from the wood and were marching in force over the plain, towards the ridge of Barrosa, and were therefore threatening his rear. Unwilling to abandon Barrosa and the small force he had left on the hill, Graham immediately gave orders to countermarch, in the hope of reinforcing Brown; but before he emerged from the wood, Marshal Victor had succeeded in driving Brown off, though in good order.

When Graham reached the open plain, the situation he had to face was critical and almost desperate. The right wing of the enemy, under Laval, was close upon him; the left, consisting of Ruffin's men, led on by Victor himself, were in possession of Barrosa; it had proved impossible, in such intricate ground, to preserve complete order in his own columns, 'and,' he adds, 'there never was time to restore it entirely.' He looked in vain for his Spanish allies. La Peña, who was responsible for the situation, made no attempt to come to the assistance of the British, or to retake Barrosa, but Graham showed no sign of hesitation. To Brown's request for orders, he had returned the single word 'Fight,' and in this spirit he determined to act, although deprived of the help on which he had relied when he began his countermarch. Retreat was, indeed, impossible, for the enemy's right wing could have intercepted them by the sea-beach, and would probably have destroyed the whole force in the confusion that must have ensued. Graham says:

> Trusting to the known heroism of British troops, regardless of the numbers and position of the enemy, an immediate attack was determined upon.

Graham's plan of battle was well conceived, and the trust he placed in his troops was amply justified. While the infantry were being formed, the artillery, under Major Duncan, opened upon the enemy a battery of ten guns. Under cover of these, the right wing was formed of the Brigade of Guards, Lieut.-Col. Brown's flank battalion of the 28th, two companies of the 2nd Rifle Corps, and a stray portion of the 67th Foot. The left was composed of Wheatley's Brigade, with three stray companies of the Coldstreams, and Barnard's flank company.

This accomplished, the advance was resumed, still under cover of the artillery, and the right wing with Dilkes in command proceeded to the assistance of Brown and the rearguard, who were in action with Ruffin at the foot of the Barrosa ridge. After a fierce and prolonged struggle, they succeeded in putting Victor's force to flight, and remained in possession of Barrosa. It is with the left wing that we are more immediately concerned. Gough and the 87th had emerged from the wood in good order, owing to a fortunate accident. A staff officer of artillery, while taking a message to another part of the field, happened to pass the battalion, and gave its commander the information that the enemy were close at hand. Gough seized an opportunity of withdrawing his regiment to a comparatively open space, where he drew it up.

On coming out of the wood, he took advantage of a chance of deploying, and was able to form in line, and to throw out his flank in view of the enemy's advance. For some time the regiment remained inactive and exposed to a galling fire, while Barnard's light troops were skirmishing in front. While thus waiting, with ordered arms, the 87th lost a major, a captain, two lieutenants, and more than fifty men. At last, the light troops were withdrawn, and the fortunes of the day depended upon one of the hand-to-hand encounters which were so frequent at this period. The 87th advanced and proceeded to charge the 8th French Regiment. The nature of the fighting is thus described by Gough, in a letter written to his wife, on the morrow of the battle:—

We proudly bring with us a trophy that will long record the result of two successive charges, against two regiments, the 8th and the 47th. The former came into the field, 1,600 grenadiers, the finest looking men I ever saw, and from the centre of their column we took their eagles. The scene in this charge was even distressing to my feelings. The French waited until we came within about 25 paces of them, before they broke, and as they were in column when they did, they could not get away. It was therefore a scene of most dreadful carnage. I will own to you my weakness. As of course I was in front of the regiment,

GENL LAVAL'S DIVIS

D'GDS.

87TH

87TH

28TH

DT

95TH

95TH

Por

3RD Pos

Pine Wood

Almanza Creek

from
Chiclana

B

C
Casa del
Peña

D

P.Bermeja

GULF O

Darbishire & StanBrd, Lttd

Scale
300   500
0

A   Hill of Barosa.
B   Graham's Division on its march to join La Peñ
C   Position of La Peña.
D   French post taken by Ladrizabal.
E   Plain on which the enemy made its appearance.

GEN⁺ RUFIN'S DIVISION

Laguna del Puerco

E

C.Browns 47OOS. DIGOS. 67TH

Walkeen Gds.

guese

tion

Position

Position

A

Vela Barosa

F.S.Corps

C.Browns 47⁰⁰⁴ 67TH DIGOS.

French Cavalry

German Cavalry

G Casa de los Guardos

To Souil

T.Barosa

CADIZ

f Yards
900   1200   1500

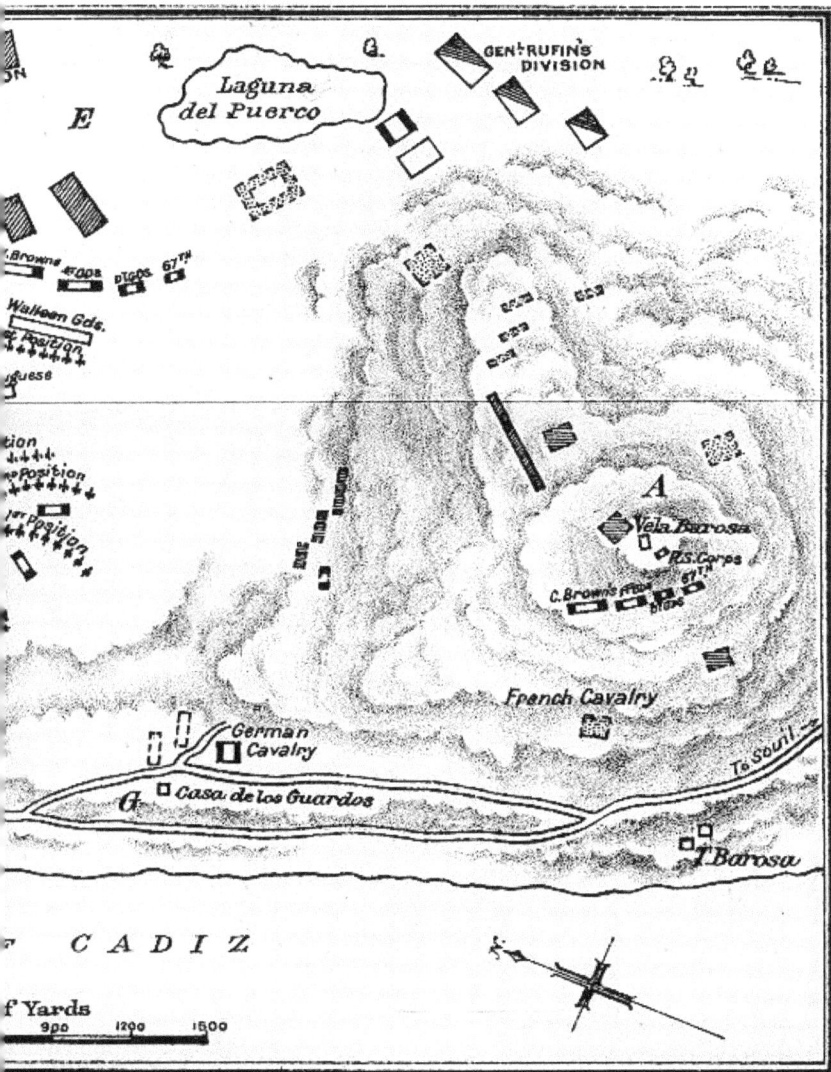

The Oxford Geog⁺ Institute.

, when the news of the enemy's approach was received.

therefore in the middle of them, I could not, confused and flying as they were, cut down one, although I thought might have twenty, they seemed so confounded and so frightened. They made, while we were amongst them (about quarter of an hour), little or no opposition.

We could have taken or destroyed the whole regiment, but at this moment the 47th French Regiment came down on our right, and General Graham, who was, during the whole of the action, in the midst of it, pointed them out and begged I would call off my men (I will not say 'Halt' as we were in the midst of the French). With the greatest difficulty by almost cutting them down, I got the right wing collected, with which we charged the 47th, but after firing until we came to within about 50 paces of them, they (for us, fortunately) broke and fled, for had they done their duty, fatigued as my men were, at the moment, they must have cut us to pieces.

We were therefore, after they broke, unable to follow them, but took the howitzer attached to them. I have ended this glorious action after two and a half hours' roar of cannon and musketry. I was fortunate in losing only one officer, four sergeants, and forty-one rank and file killed; Major Maclaine severely, Captain Somersall severely, Lts. Barton and Fennell both severely, six sergeants and 121 rank and file, wounded.

★★★★★★

Note:—The memoirs of the colonel of the 8th French Regiment (Vigo-Roussillon) have been published in the *Revue des Deux Mondes*, July-August, 1891. He states that, just before his regiment was charged by the 87th, he had an opportunity of slaying General Graham. He was not aware of Graham's identity, but he refrained, owing to his venerable appearance and natural dignity. '*Son sang-froid, un grand air de calme et de dignité, avaient arrêté mon bras.*' Almost immediately he was himself wounded, and it was while he was wounded that the 87th routed his regiment and captured the eagle. '*Les Testes de mon bataillon, se voyant sur le point d'être entourés, reculèrent, et une charge vigoureuse, faite, de nouveau, par le 87e régiment anglais, acheva de les rompre . . . Dans la dernière charge le porte-aigle du 1er bataillon ayant été tué, les Anglais s'étaient emparés de cette aigle. Bien des braves se dévouèrent pour la reprendre et trouvèrent ainsi une mort glorieuse. Cette aigle coûta cher aux Anglais, beaucoup de leurs officiers payèrent de leur vie l'honneur de la conserver, mais enfin, elle leur resta.'*

Vigo-Roussillon describes how he surrendered to an officer, who saved him from the attack of a sergeant; the latter not perceiving his wounded condition. This incident is probably the origin of the legend that Gough decapitated the colonel of a French regiment at Barrosa. Writing many years later, with reference to newspaper tales. Lord Gough said:

> 'I was once the white-headed boy who cut off the head of the French Colonel at Barosa, who was at the very time of his decapitation quietly amusing himself at Paris.'

He seems to have been in error in imagining that Vigo-Roussillon was not on the field—unless, indeed, the myth has a different origin altogether.

★★★★★★

The charge of the 87th, aided by the three companies of Guards, who shared in the honour of the onslaught, and supported by the remainder of the wing, decided the fate of Laval's troops. No serious attempt to rally was made by the French wings, and Graham was left in possession of the field. (There is an interesting account of the Battle of Barrosa in *Light Bob,* by Robert Blakeny).

The battle had unquestionably been gained by the courage of the British troops, and in spite of the culpable negligence of the Spaniards, to whose disgraceful conduct Byron alluded in the well-known lines:—

Bear witness, bright Barrosa, thou canst tell
Whose were the sons that bravely fought and fell.

Graham, however, does full justice to such assistance as the allies actually rendered. The junction with Zayas was effected by Lardizabal only after some hard fighting; two Spanish battalions, which had been left on the hill, ignoring La Peña's order to retire, returned to strengthen the right wing of the British; and General Whittingham, an Englishman, in command of the Spanish cavalry, while not taking advantage of the opportunity of making a flank attack on Ruffin, did keep in check a corps of infantry and cavalry which endeavoured to turn the position of the Barrosa height, by means of the beach road. Busch and his hussars also made a gallant charge and routed a squadron of French dragoons.

Nothing, indeed, can be urged in extenuation of the conduct of La Peña. He did not inform Graham of his intention to abandon Barrosa, and betake himself, by the beach, to Santi Petri; but even if Graham had understood this, it could not palliate La Peña's desertion of his allies when the French attacked. Nor did his supineness end here. The British troops, which had been under arms for over twenty-four hours, were too much exhausted by the fighting to be able to follow up their victory with an onslaught upon the retreating French Army. La Peña, with more than twelve thousand fresh troops, maintained his attitude of cowardly inactivity, and Graham could do nothing but withdraw the greater portion of his army to the Isla de Leon.

★★★★★★

Note:—Where the account of the Battle of Barrosa, as given above, differs from the description in Napier's *Peninsular War* (bk. xi. chap. 2), it is based upon Gough MSS. and upon Graham's dispatches. Napier seems to have overstated the disorder of Graham's force, when he wrote of the troops under Wheatley and Dilkes as forming 'two masses, without any attention to regiments or brigades.' Some statements in Napier's first edition which were clearly erroneous were modified in subsequent editions, in deference to a protest made by Gough on the appearance of Napier's book. Napier's inaccurate statements, with regard to Barrosa, and afterwards in connexion with the siege of Tarifa, are probably responsible for the error sometimes made of attaching the soubriquet, '*Faugh-a-Ballaghs*' (Clear the ways), to the 88th or the 89th instead of to the 87th Regiment, to which alone it is historically applicable.

★★★★★★

The desertion of La Peña, while it diminished the effect of the victory, could not but add to its glory. What might easily have been a disaster of great moment had been converted into an overwhelming victory. An eagle and six pieces of cannon were among the spoils of the day. Ruffin was a prisoner, and the French loss in killed and wounded was very great. When the news of Graham's gallant and successful attack, against an enemy of such superior numbers and possessed of the key of the position, reached Great Britain, it was received with an enthusiasm which was out of proportion to the intrinsic importance of the incident, though amply deserved by the heroism of Graham and his men. Lord Liverpool, in his dispatch to General Graham, gave utterance to the public feeling when he wrote:—

The memory of those who conquered and of those who fell

in the hour of victory upon the Height of Barrosa will be ever cherished by the British nation, and their names will hold a conspicuous rank amongst the bravest and worthiest of our heroes.

The thanks of both Houses of Parliament were conveyed to General Graham and his army, and newspaper columns overflowed with tributes in prose and verse, while audiences at the London theatres sang:—

> *They tell us that Eagles can stare at the sun,*
> *Whose beams nor annoy nor dismay 'em;*
> *But French Eagles fly and French Game Chickens run.*
> *From the glory of General Graham,*

The 87th had its due share of the glory, as it had its share of the fighting. The Eagle which they had captured was the first taken in the war, and further interest attached to it from the fact that the laurel wreath which surmounted it was the gift of Napoleon himself, and that Napoleon's confidence in the 8th Regiment was so great that, by his special orders, the eagle was not attached to the standard in the ordinary way. There was some curiosity about it in England, and Gough gave the following description of it, in answer to a query of his wife:

> It is brass, well gilt; the wreath is pure gold. The eagle was on a pole, something stronger, but very similar to the pole of a sergeant's halbert. It is much heavier than the colours of a regiment, and from the weight being all at the top, is very unwieldy.

Graham was fully conscious of the importance of the two great charges made by the 87th. He mentioned them with special commendation in his dispatch, and wrote to the Colonel, Sir John Doyle:

> Your regiment has covered itself with glory. Recommend it, and its commander, to their illustrious patron, the Prince Regent; too much cannot be done for it.

The result of these recommendations was that the 87th was honoured by the prince regent with the title of the Prince of Wales's Own Irish Regiment; and it was allowed to bear 'as a badge of honour upon the regimental colours and appointments an eagle with a wreath of laurel above the harp, in addition to the arms of His Royal Highness.' Gough had been particularly mentioned in Graham's dispatch and 'earnestly recommended' for promotion, and he immediately received the brevet rank of Lieutenant-Colonel On the recommendation of

BATTLE OF
BARROSA
5th March 1811.

SCALES
Cavalry   Allies Infantry   French
French Artillery

Retreat of the French

VIGIA DE LA BARROSA

ATLANTIC OCEAN

RIO DE SANTI PETRI

the Duke of Wellington, the brevet rank was, as we shall see, subsequently antedated from Barrosa to the date of Wellington's dispatches relative to the Battle of Talavera. This is the first instance, in the history of the British Army, of the conferment of brevet rank upon an officer for the conduct of a regiment in action.

The captured eagle was conveyed to England, and presented to the prince regent, and its arrival caused fresh public interest in the Prince's Own, which for the time occupied the position of the popular regiment.

★★★★★★

Note:—The eagle was placed in the chapel of Chelsea Hospital, where it remained till the 16th April, 1852, when it was stolen, The staff was sawn through, and the Eagle removed—whether by a patriotic Frenchman, or by a thief who thought the eagle was made of gold, has never been discovered. A facsimile is now in Chelsea Hospital.

★★★★★★

Its health was proposed by the Lord Mayor at a City of London banquet, at which Doyle modestly disclaimed for his regiment anything but 'superior good fortune in retaining the trophies they had won.' The regimental songs of the period are full of the new honours conferred upon the regiment, and express appropriate devotion to the prince regent:—

And life, that's a debt paid to nature by others,
We brought a free gift to the prince we obey.

★★★★★★

Note:—Some claim to the honour of capturing the Eagle was made by another corps, and elicited a protest from Gough, who says: 'Ensign Keogh was killed in the act of grasping at it, and the French officer who held it was ran through by Sergeant Masterson in the midst of our officers and men. This sergeant never let it out of his hand until he delivered it to me, and afterwards carried it the remainder of the day between our colours.' The claim of the 87th was undeniable, and the slight difficulty that arose was caused by the fact that three companies of the Guards, under Colonel Jackson, charged on the left of the 87th, and in the confusion of the onslaught spectators did not distinguish between the different corps. A leaf of the laurel wreath round the neck of the Eagle, which was loose when it was captured, was sent by Gough to his wife, and is still preserved, with other relics of the campaign, at Lough Cutra Castle.

✦✦✦✦✦✦

Brilliant as was the victory, the Battle of Barrosa is more properly regarded as an escape from a terrible disaster than as an important turning-point in a campaign. Graham's intention was, as we have pointed out, to raise the siege of Cadiz. Had he been enthusiastically or even decently supported by the Spaniards, his purpose would probably have been accomplished. As it was he inflicted a grave blow, physical and moral, upon the French, and saved himself and La Peña from a crushing defeat; if not, indeed, from a massacre. But the siege of Cadiz was renewed; and the main object of Graham's bold move had not been attained.

La Pena's misconduct was not confined to cowardice. He had the effrontery to claim the credit of the victory for himself, and an angry controversy ensued, which rendered it impossible for Graham to continue to act with the Spanish commander, and led, ultimately, to the transference of his services to another portion of the field. From the Cortes, which had appointed La Peña, and which retained him in his command, Graham refused to accept any honour.

So slight had been the effect of the victory of Barrosa upon the course of the blockade, that Victor's operations seem never to have been interrupted. On the 24th of March, Gough writes:

> We are all getting on here as you might expect. The Spaniards have all run away, and the bridge over the Santi Petri is broken down. There was a most heavy cannonade last night. I have not as yet heard the result. The last one of this sort, when upwards of forty shells were thrown into Cadiz, it is now ascertained, actually killed a cat. Whether any of that species of Spaniard suffered last night, I know not.

The continued shelling of Cadiz may have been alarming to the shipping in the harbour, but it did not arrest the flow of spirits among the British troops in the Isla, who celebrated the arrival of dispatches from home, dealing with the Battle of Barrosa, by feasts and merriment. Gough says:

> I was obliged to give all the officers a let-off, several friends dined with me, and a hundred and four bottles of wine were drunk. (Letter of April 24, 1811).

64

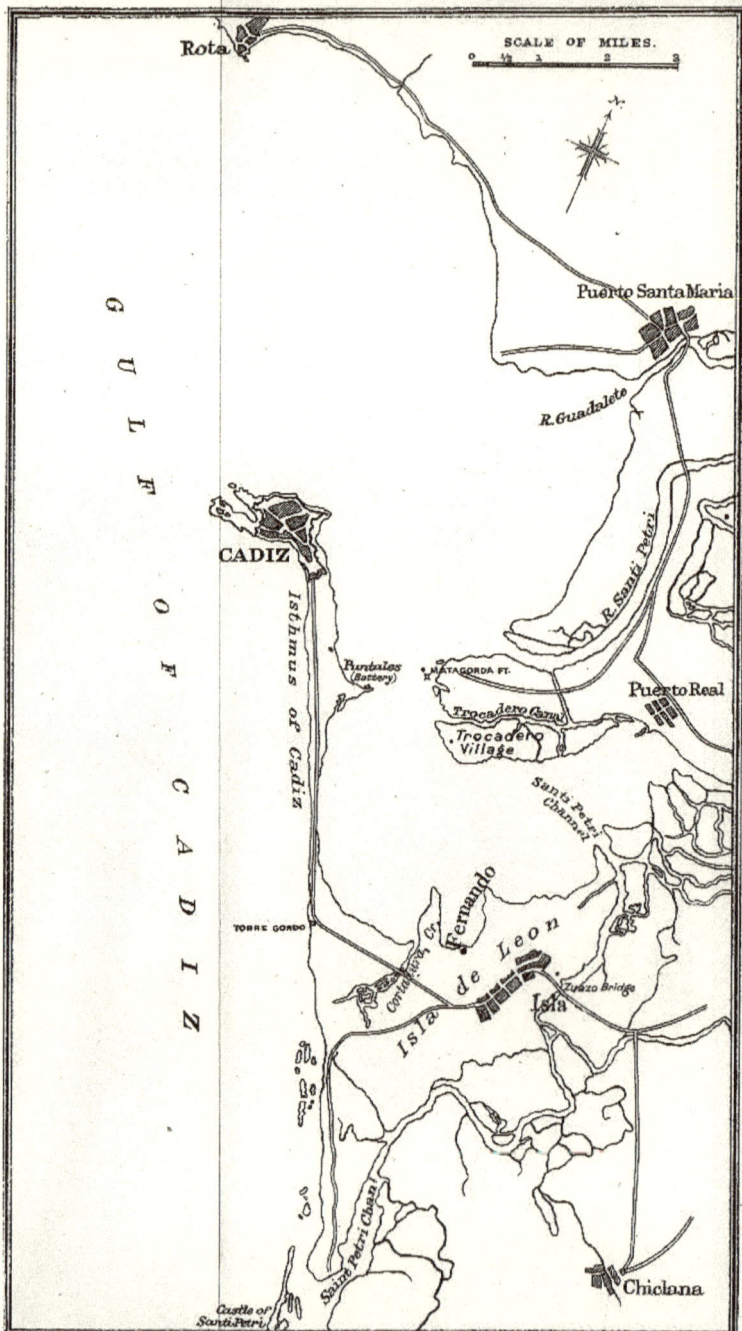

Rota

SCALE OF MILES.

0 ½ 1 2 3

Puerto Santa Maria

R. Guadalete

R. Santi Petri

CADIZ

Isthmus of Cadiz

Puntales
(Battery)

MATAGORDA FT.

Puerto Real

Trocadero Canal

Trocadero Village

Santi Petri Channel

TORRE GORDO

Cortadura Cr.

Fernando

Isla de Leon

Zuazo Bridge

Isla

Santi Petri Channel

Castle of
Santi Petri

Chiclana

The 87th remained in the Isla from the date of Barrosa till the end of May, when they were sent into garrison at Cadiz. For about six months, the battalion is almost always in one or other of these two positions. In June we find Gough back again in the Isla, in July he is in Cadiz, in August there is a slight change to San Roque, and so on, until the month of October, when a more serious movement fell to his lot.

2: Cadiz and Tarifa

The six months which intervened between the battle of Barrosa and the beginning of the siege of Tarifa (the next incident in the war which concerns us closely) were full of notable events in other regions of the Peninsula. The construction of the lines of Torres Vedras, in the winter of 1809-10, had, in the ensuing summer, kept Massena at bay, and, by the date of Barrosa, had resulted in his retreat from Portugal. He was followed by Wellington, whose army had now received sufficient reinforcements to enable him to adopt offensive measures. In May, Wellington defeated Massena at Fuentes d'Onoro, and a few days later the troops under Beresford were successful at Albuera. Meanwhile, there fell to the lot of the garrison at Cadiz only such domestic incidents as relieve the monotony of life in a blockaded town. The blockade continued throughout the summer and autumn, and not even the defeat of Albuera compelled Soult to withdraw his troops from Cadiz. To the conduct of Soult during the summer campaign of 1811, Napier pays a well-deserved tribute;

> When unexpectedly assailed by Beresford from the north, by the Murcians on the east, by Ballesteros on the west, by Graham and La Peña in the south, he found means to repel three of those attacks, to continue the blockade of Cadiz, and to keep Seville tranquil, while he marched against the fourth.

The command of the sea, retained by the British, saved the blockaded troops from any of the real hardships of a siege, and they seem to have suffered chiefly from tedium. Gough's correspondence is full of the usual gossip of the mess-room.

> Reports here are so numerous, and in general so ill-founded, that it is impossible to give credit to anything you hear.

When he has a real piece of news to record, it is not always of a pleasant nature. He writes, on June the 29th:

> Our revered general leaves us tomorrow for Portugal, as second in command. This distressing piece of news reached us the day before yesterday. I immediately waited on him to say the whole corps entreated he would take a farewell dinner with us. With tears in his eyes (I own I could not avoid shedding some), he fixed on this day, although he said he had made a resolution not to dine out. He has refused every other person and corps. Never did I see such universal regret, even the rascally Spaniards seem to feel the loss they will have in Graham. He takes all his staff with him. Major General Cooke succeeds.

Gough's love for Graham led him to entertain the hope of obtaining permission to accompany him to Portugal, although he had just received the command of a brigade at Cadiz; but he had to dismiss the idea as quite out of the question while the blockade lasted. The weariness of enforced idleness led him to make various plans for the future. The warmth of his home affections suggested schemes for obtaining leave.

> If nothing is to be done here, and I vow I see not the slightest chance of it, I propose in November getting nine months leave.

Again he thinks he would be better in active work at home than idle at Cadiz, and speculates on the chance of being made Adjutant-General at Limerick or at Athlone. In a letter from Cadiz he gives a description of his monotonous day. (Letter of August 9, 1811).

> I get up at five, walk about two miles to the sea to bathe; after returning, I have just time to dress for my Parade at eight, which I dismiss at ten, breakfast, and read till twelve, from which hour to one I give up to the interior of the regiment, at my desk. I now lie down for an hour and a half, get up and dress for dinner at three. I generally take the first allowance, a pint, which, with chatting to, I believe, an attached set of brother officers, brings me to five, at which hour my horse is at the door, and from which I ride until half-past seven. It is by this time getting dark. I then devote one hour to contemplation, strolling on an eminence near my quarters. You may well conceive where my thoughts wander. I transport myself to Plymouth, and almost in idea then feel all the joys I should there experience. From nine

to ten I read, when I look round to see everything quiet, and retire to a solitary bed—my only wish either to forget I am in it or to sleep for the purpose of dreaming of all my soul holds most dear. In this account of one day and night, you nearly perceive how I pass my time.

A month later, it is the same story:—

I wish of all things to go to Portugal. . . . I am sick to death of this town. . . . Anything is better than this dull, stupid place and way of spending one's time.'

There was certainly no special reason for loving Cadiz or its people. The dispute between Graham and the Spanish Government about the responsibility for the failure at Barrosa added to the indignation felt against La Peña, and reports,(quoted in Napier vol. iii.), from Cadiz in the course of the summer are full of the jealousy which subsisted between the allied forces, and of the weakness and misrule of the Spanish Regency.

The temper of the public mind at Cadiz is very bad, the press has lately teemed with publications filled with reproaches of the English. . . . The Regency and Cortes have lost all influence everywhere . . . the Spanish generals have been quarrelling.

Six weeks before leaving Cadiz, Graham wrote:—

The government here supported by the Cortes seemed to be determined to adhere with blind obstinacy and pride to a system that has nearly brought the cause to ruin, and notwithstanding Lord Wellington's great efforts they are playing Buonaparte's game so positively that I despair of any great good.'
A report written on the last day of July sums up the situation:—
'Nothing can be more wretched than the state of affairs here; the regents are held in universal contempt, and such is the want of talent, I can hardly hope that a change will make any improvement: the treasury is empty, and no probability of the arrival of any money from America, so that affairs are really in a worse state than they have been at any time since the commencement of the war.

October brought a welcome relief. After the Battle of Barrosa, Brown had returned to Tarifa, and remained in command of the garrison till the end of June, when he left, with the 28th Regiment, to join Wellington. He was succeeded by Major King, of the 82nd, who, in spite of the complete quiet which had persisted through the summer, insisted upon the improvement of the defences. In the middle of August, some alarm was caused by the siege of the neighbouring castle of Alcala by a French Army, and General Beguines represented that Tarifa was the real object of attack. Lieutenant-General Campbell prepared a plan for the defence, which was carried out under King. In the beginning of September, the aspect of affairs became more threatening. Soult, who seems to have aimed at using Tarifa as a depot for the army at Cadiz, drove Ballesteros to seek shelter under the guns of Gibraltar, but want of provisions caused him to withdraw, and Ballesteros escaped.

On the 22nd, the garrison of Alcala surrendered, and although Ballesteros won a small victory three days later, the British commandant at Tarifa decided that reinforcements must immediately be obtained. The jealousy of the general in command of the Spanish troops (Don Manuel Daban) caused some opposition, but the wisdom of King's demand was justified when Ballesteros was again driven back upon Gibraltar, by the enemy's occupation of San Roque. In answer to king's request, it was decided to send twelve hundred men to Tarifa, and among the troops selected for this purpose was the 2nd Battalion of the 87th, whose commander thus describes their start:—

Off Tarifa: Oct 12th, 1811.
It seemed the enemy threatened the Spanish General Ballesteros, and General Cooke has thought it advisable to send a force to Tarifa to attract their attention to that quarter, thereby to save this last hope of the Spanish cause, the aforementioned Spanish General. But I believe, indeed I am certain, that Colonel Skerrett, of the 47th, who has got the command, has likewise the most positive orders not to attempt anything offensive, and to fall back immediately the object will be gained by drawing the French force towards the North, where we are to act. Indeed, when I mention our force, it will prove to you that we have not been sent to fight, as it only consists of a light brigade of artillery, under Captain Hughes, eight companies of the 47th regiment (550) under Major Broad, eight companies of the 87th (525), and one company of the 95th under Capt. Jenkins (75)—in all no more than 1,200 men. Colonel Skerrett 1st in command with Lieutenant Colonel Lord Proby of the guards,

2nd, your humble servant, the next senior officer.

I cannot tell you the delight this little temporary move has given us all, anything for a change to a soldier. . . . We only got the first intimation of such a thing going forward while I was at dinner on the 9th, and at ten next morning I marched down to the Malle and embarked the whole of the men and baggage in three minutes, to the astonishment of every person present. The Captain-of-the-Navy Bruce, who, by the bye, tells me he knows you very well, said at a public dinner that day, before the commanding officers of the other corps, that, since he came into the Navy, he never saw a regiment embark in the enthusiastic style the 87th did, which by the bye was true, as I never saw such a set of fellows, it really is a pity that they will be disappointed in not meeting the enemy, and will you excuse me for adding that I regret it also! If, however, that time will arrive, whether they succeed or otherwise, they will do themselves honour and their country service. It really is a sin they are not in Portugal and not employed in this dirty little peddling warfare.

Captain Dickson commands the naval part of the expedition, who I will forward my letters through. You must still continue to direct to me at Cadiz; we will be back long ere this reaches you. Let me entreat you not to mind what you may see in the papers about us, you know there is no dependence to be placed on their reports. As we will not march more than a league or two from Tarifa (which bye the bye you know is a small walled town at the entrance of the Straights of Gibraltar) you may always depend on hearing everything from me. You know my promise to tell you nothing but truth, which I shall be the more determined in, from my knowledge that your good sense would convince you that, was I even in what is called danger, that a hair of my head cannot fall to the ground without the consent and will of the great Disposer of events. . . . We are now beating about in the mouth of the Gut of Gibraltar, but as the wind is from the Eastward we shall not arrive at all events before tomorrow morning.

Tarifa: October 16th.

After six days most boisterous passage, we reached this place last night and landed this morning—with the exception of a part of my Lt. Company under Thompson, and half number 8 under Waller, who, together with our brigade of guns, are missing. We cannot conjecture what has become of them. We have everything here quiet, but the French about 8,000, have driven Ballesteros under the guns of Gibraltar, and have taken up their position at Saint Roque. There are none in our neighbourhood and we have advanced reconnoitring parties to Algesiras. Since we were here last they have strengthened this place much, and I much apprehend after the enemy have eaten up all the provisions of the neighbourhood they will retire. Indeed it can be no object for them to remain where they are— their stay will, however, protract the time of our returning. We have found a British force here of 400 men from Gibraltar.

The general course of events may be gathered from the following passages, selected from Colonel Gough's letters of the period:—

Tarifa: 18th October,
We yesterday made a reconnaissance towards Algesiras, where we found the enemy had evacuated that town and fallen back on their force at Saint Roque. We today move a few miles in the other direction, to drive back a small division of five or six hundred men they have about three leagues from this for the purpose of watching our movements. Or at least I presume this is our intention. I wish Colonel Skerrett would leave the business to the Prince's Own. But as a married man I shall never volunteer this, much as I may wish little affairs of this kind. As I flatter myself, though little as my loss would be to others, there is one dear friend in England who, as she is everything to me, I am equally the world to her. We will therefore act, I presume, as it was said of the King of France who had fifty thousand men, 'marched them up the hill and down again.'

Tarifa: 19th (October)
We have been moving up the hill, and down again these two days, without doing anything but fagging the men. Had we had good information yesterday, and a little dash, we could have done a very pretty thing. . . . Oh! for a Graham—this is the country for such characters. . . .

Tarifa: 22nd (October)
I am most happy to announce that the object of our expedition is accomplished, and that we only now wait the return of

73

a vessel from Cadiz to go back. The day before yesterday, we marched out to a position 15 miles from this, close to 2,000 of the enemy: a plain divided us. We formed and offered them battle, which they declined, and we returned that night after a most distressing march. The enemy, on our evacuating the position, took it up; but yesterday morning their whole force retired to their former position towards Ronda. . . . I will own I hardly expected so fortunate a result, from the smallness of our force, and other causes. The enemy must have been much deceived, or they have had some other motive than dread from us.

By the end of October, Gough considered that their work was done, he writes:

The enemy have evacuated this part of the country. We only await letters from General Cooke to return.

But he was fated to see considerably more of the 'most wretched little village in Europe.'

Tarifa: November 11th, 1811.
When I sent off my last journal (the 2nd *ultimo*) I then expected we should have been long ere this period at Cadiz, but circumstances, principally foul winds and the different movements of the Spanish Armies in this part of the kingdom, have, and probably will, detain us for some time. We have had some severe marches to favour the movements of Ballesteros, who hangs on the rear of the enemy before Cadiz. On the sixth we marched 42 miles and took, without bloodshed, Vejer, a town situated on the summit of an almost perpendicular mountain. The enemy had about 250 men who, after firing a few long (very long indeed) shots at the Spaniards, fell back to Chiclana. Every man should have been taken and the relief that came to their assistance (of the same strength) but for the stupidity, or any other worse name you may please to call it, of the Spanish General (Copons) who commanded.
We returned to this town to refresh the men two days back. I should have been very sick of the whole business, had I not had an opportunity of going over on the 1st of November to Tangiers for twenty four hours. We were only three hours crossing over and five coming back. I was most pleasingly undeceived with regard to the Moors. They are an uncommon fine race

of men (the ladies are not visible), and in my humble opinion deserve the name of savages quite as little as the lower order of Spaniards, or I will add, my own countrymen.

I was very fortunate in seeing everything worth seeing in the place. Nothing was ever so cheap as are all articles in Tangiers; my whole days expense was for eating and drinking a dollar and a half, including port wine, &c.

In the middle of November, the enemy unexpectedly reappeared, and a fruitless expedition followed, of which Gough wrote an account to his wife on the 23rd:—

Your most kind letter of the 17th October reached me most opportunely the 18th . . . after being most disappointed the day previous, when we had an opportunity of reacting the scene of Barrosa, and when, had we had but a Graham, another day glorious to the British arms would have taken place. We marched from this on the 12th for the purpose of making a diversion in favour of Ballesteros, and for three days hurried in rear of the enemy before Cadiz, one day threatening this, another that, point of their defence.

On the 17th, when at Vejer, the enemy most unexpectedly made his appearance; our look-out was so bad and our reconnoitring so infamous that their Columns came within gunshot before it was even known they were in the neighbourhood. I, fortunately, returning from the town of Vejer . . . perceived some of the enemy's dragoons, and not having the highest opinion of those with whom I was acting, after I gave directions for the men to be ready to fall in at a moment's notice, proceeded to a hill from which I could perceive any body of men advancing. I had nearly reached the summit when I saw the enemy on a hill within a mile and a half, who had by this time evidently made their dispositions of attack and were pushing forward with all the French vivacity of attack.

Bright was with me. I ordered him down the hill to put the brigade under arms, while I waited to reconnoitre their movements. A few minutes decided their evident point of attack. . . . They advanced in three columns, in all consisting of apparently, to me, 2,000 (we have since ascertained 2,250), three hundred of whom were cavalry, and 2 field-pieces. We had 1,030 infantry, 49 cavalry, and 4 field-pieces, with good management a very strong position; there could not for a moment be a doubt of what should be done. On joining the brigade, I found myself senior officer. Colonel Skerret and Lord Proby being absent. I immediately proceeded to put in execution (or, rather was going, as the whole of the men were not under arms, when I joined them) that plan, not of defence, but of attack, that appeared from their movements almost certain of success (and which the senior officer of engineers has since told me would be the plan he would and did advise), but at this moment our commander made his appearance, and ordered me to march. . . . We formed on a hill in the rear, until the lt. company which was in the town, and who were sharply engaged with the two strongest columns, but were obliged for want of support to fall back with the remainder of the light companies, rejoined us, Somersal was so hard pushed that he was forced to leave all his knapsacks.

One sergeant could not be got to fall back, and was taken, and one more wounded. The whole brigade fell back to the position of Vacinos that evening, and two days back returned to this town. To do Colonel Skerret justice, I believe he had orders not to fight superior numbers, and Vejer is within a few hours march of the lines at Cadiz, where the enemy have 14,000 men; but if a man does not venture, he will never win. We would have beaten them with very little loss, and we could then have fallen back.

Those who wish to vindicate the propriety of not fighting say: What object would you have gained? My answer and I think the answer of every British soldier would be: We would have supported the character of the British arms, which by falling back before a force but double our numbers is in a measure injured.'

The incident was trivial, but the letter is of some interest, not merely as throwing light on the character of the writer, but as indicating the courage and confidence with which Wellington had inspired the British forces in the Peninsula. Gough expected to return immediately to Cadiz; but, as will be seen from the letter which follows, it was decided to form a junction with Ballesteros, and the brigade was sent to Gibraltar. The enemy took advantage of their absence to menace Tarifa, and the design had to be given up.

Tarifa: December 10th, 1811.

Your affectionately kind letter of the 3rd November I received on the 4th, but so fagged have we been since marching, that I really am half dead. Since my last we have been at Gibraltar; indeed there are few places many leagues from this that we have not visited.

The enemy have again driven Ballesteros under the guns of Gibraltar. We marched to Algesiras, and crossed over by night for the purpose of attacking their position at Saint Rosque together with 5,000 Spaniards, but that morning Suchet, (this is probably a slip of the pen for Soult, as Suchet was near Valencia at this time), joined the enemy with 3,000, making in all 12,000, and the project was immediately given up, as we had but a 1,000 British, and the Spaniards were a most wretched rabble. The enemy had menaced this place and have marched to Vacinos, twelve miles off, 2,300 men and a few pieces of ordnance. Two days back they pushed forward some men within sight of the town which so frightened the natives that a sight most melancholy, though ludicrous, occurred; women and children running through the streets with as much of their property as they could carry for the purpose of embarking for Ceuta.

But on finding the enemy had retired several have again come on shore. I am fully persuaded they never for a moment seriously thought of attacking this place. I am equally certain their object is to detain us here until they find an opportunity of attacking either Ballesteros or Blake. Their force is so totally inadequate even to resisting us in the field. We have been however hourly, day and night, employed in strengthening the place, fagging the men and officers to death. . . . They must either advance or retire in a day or two.

13th. The enemy, with the exception of a few men, have retired to Vejer, so all apprehension of an attack on this place is over for the winter; indeed the weather has been so dreadful that it was impossible for them to have remained; the inhabitants have therefore all again returned to the town. I therefore hope we shall shortly go back.

The words with which this letter closes should, probably, not be taken too seriously as expressing the real views of the writer, for the obvious intention is to avoid alarming Mrs. Gough; but it is, at the same time, evident that the next movement of the enemy was a surprise to the garrison. On the 16th, a general order was issued, warning the forces that an attack was imminent, and on the 18th there was actually a cavalry skirmish. It is not necessary to follow the series of skirmishes which followed, nor to trace the French manoeuvres in detail, as they drew their lines closer round the town. At this stage of the blockade, there could scarcely be any doubt as to the real intention of the French, and the anonymous 'British Officer in Garrison,' who wrote *Anecdotes of British and Spanish Heroism at Tarifa, in Spain* (Lond., 1812), on which we largely rely for details of the fighting, states that a French sergeant, captured on the 22nd, reported that the French were determined to take the town.

'Tis a positive order from Napoleon, our emperor, that we should do so; and he generally provides means adequate to the end.

In two letters written home, on the 23rd and the 29th, Gough continues to hide from his wife the real danger of the situation.

The enemy finding they can get no good of Ballesteros, have given up keeping him under the guns of Gibraltar, and have come before us to play the same game they have been doing these last two years at Cadiz. They yesterday advanced and invested the town in form, they have brought nothing but a few light guns. Their object, I am persuaded, is merely to get Ballesteros away from Gibraltar. Here they cannot long remain, and even should they, it is as good to be shut up in one town as in another. I much fear as this is a new thing, they will frighten you with newspaper accounts, as they first did about Cadiz.

Before these words were written (on the 29th), Gough had already taken his part in the momentous decision as to the defence of the town, which led to one of the most honourable episodes in the Peninsular War. At this point, it is essential for the proper appreciation of the work done by the 87th, to turn to an account of the situation and defences of the fortress of Tarifa.

Situated almost in the centre of the Spanish side of the Straits of Gibraltar, Tarifa is naturally a place of considerable importance, and has a long history. It takes its name from a Saracen soldier, Tarif, and its associations with the struggle between the Cross and the Crescent are further increased by 'the tower of the Guzmans,' to which we shall have to make reference, and which recalls a famous siege in 1294, when the Spanish governor, Guzman, saved Tarifa from the Moors. In later history, Tarifa acquired an unenviable reputation as a home of pirates, and during the wars between Great Britain and Spain, in the eighteenth century, it was the scene of numerous privateering attacks upon British shipping.

At the beginning of the Peninsular War, it was thought undesirable to attempt to hold Tarifa, and the town was in the occasional occupation of the enemy, who used it as a base for cattle-snatching expeditions. In May, 1809, General Colin Campbell, (not the future Lord Clyde, who was at this date a lieutenant, and in that capacity fought both at Barrosa and at Tarifa), who was in command at Gibraltar, sent to Tarifa a detachment, which, by subsequent additions, grew into the garrison (under Brown) of which we have already spoken in connexion with the battle of Barrosa. At the date of the attack which it is now our duty to relate, the strength of Colonel Skerrett's garrison amounted to about 2,500 (including 600 Spanish infantry and 100 horse), and the enemy numbered probably about 5,000 men. (The numbers of the French are very variously stated; cf. Napier's Appendix on the siege of Tarifa. The number we have taken is that given by Wellington in his *Dispatch*. The evidence is conflicting on a number of points in connexion with the siege).

Tarifa itself was a small town of about six thousand inhabitants. It was surrounded by a narrow wall, too weak to form any defence against artillery, but broken by a series of towers, of which the most important were the tower and castle of the Guzmans, and the Portcullis. These stand at opposite ends of the bed of a periodical torrent, which bisected the town, passing from east to southwest. What may, for convenience' sake, be termed the Portcullis, stood at the entrance of this bed, and consisted of a tower defended by a portcullis and by a series of palisades.

The tower of the Guzmans was at the south-west corner of the town, near the egress of the torrent, and the castle of the Guzmans to the east of the tower, forming part of the south wall of the town. The bed of the torrent, after passing out of the town near the south west corner, is continued, in a westerly direction, to the sea, leaving a small neck of land between itself and the straits. On the Catalina, a small sandhill on this neck of land, was a 12-pounder, covering a short causeway which led to the island of Juniana. On this small island, which extends into the Straits, were four 24-pounders, and some other pieces of artillery, but they were not all mounted in time to be of use in the siege.

On the east and north, the town was commanded by some hills, of which the enemy were in possession, and which the garrison could not hope to hold. The plan of the defence, as devised by the engineers to whom Campbell had entrusted the task, was to concentrate the fighting upon the east side. The enemy might be naturally supposed to be likely to make an attempt on the east, because the hills at that point came nearer to the walls than elsewhere. The apparent advantage thus given was more than counterbalanced by other considerations. In the first place, the ridges themselves made a natural glacis at such an angle as to expose the assault to the full effect of the fire from the defenders' musketry.

Secondly, the walls and towers were stronger at that side, and, at the same time, because of the natural features of the town, presented an appearance of weakness. The bed of the torrent almost bisected the east side of the wall, and from the Portcullis there stretched into the town a series of houses rising from both sides of the bed at an inclined plane. The existence of the torrent rendered the inner side of the wall much higher than the outer, and the houses formed a barricade on each side. If the enemy should succeed in effecting an entrance at this point, they would, accordingly, find themselves shut up in the bed of the torrent and exposed not merely to fire from the houses by which they were enclosed, but also from the tower of the Guzmans at the opposite end of the town. This tower, further, offered a point for the final resistance, and from it the garrison could, if necessary, make their way to the island.

The steps taken to induce the French to make their attack at this seemingly favourable position were, like the scheme itself, the work of Captain Smith and his engineers. The western front was strengthened so as to produce an appearance of great difficulty. Should the enemy make an effort there, they would find an outwork in the shape of a convent about a hundred yards from the northwest angle of the town. To the south were the tower of the Guzmans and the Catalina, and in the channel were a ship of the line, a frigate, and some gunboats.

The real attack commenced on the 19th of December, when the enemy took possession of the hills surrounding Tarifa. Next day, the garrison made a sally and drew the enemy towards the eastern wall of the town. Before nightfall the town was closely invested, but the enemy had suffered considerably, especially from the two 10-inch mortars on the island. On the 22nd there took place a skirmish of considerable importance. A French piquet had taken up a position to the west of the town, from which it was necessary to dislodge them. A light company of the 11th accomplished this, but under their leader. Captain Wren, were forced to retire by a part of the right wing of the French, which advanced close to the convent. The artillery, not only of the garrison, but also of some gunboats in the harbour, was directed against them; but it was also desirable to charge them, and Skerrett sent the following message to Gough:

> Dear Gough, The enemy have sent a large force in front of the convent. Be prepared for an attack on that side.

The little scrap of paper, torn off a sheet, has been preserved through all the years that have intervened since the siege of Tarifa, and it is reproduced in this book, as a relic of a famous siege.

COLONEL SKERRETT'S NOTE TO GOUGH

Gough's reply to the note was a charge with a flank company of the 87th, which forced the French to abandon their position, and relieved the garrison from the danger of allowing a hill on the west of the town to pass into the possession of the enemy.

By the morning of the 24th it was clear that the enemy had decided to attack on the east, as Smith had anticipated. At daybreak, they had pushed their advance to within 400 yards of the northeast tower. But here Colonel Skerrett lost heart. The enemy greatly outnumbered the men at his disposal, and they were determined, at all hazards, to storm the town. Neither he nor his commander, General Cooke, was responsible for the attempt to hold the place; the original occupation, and the defence, were alike the conception of the governor of the neighbouring fortress of Gibraltar.

Skerrett had always been doubtful of the possibility of holding out, and had applied to Cooke for orders. In reply, he received, on the 24th, instructions to embark his brigade and return to Cadiz. That night a council of war was held; Colonel Skerrett strongly advocated

81

the abandonment of Tarifa, and found some support for his view. It is only due to Skerrett to admit that he had considerable ground for his hesitation. Wellington, writing after the successful defence, remarked:

> We have a right to expect that his Majesty's officers and troops will perform their duty upon every occasion; but we have no right to expect that comparatively a small number would be able to hold the town of Tarifa, commanded as it is at short distances, and enfiladed in every direction, and unprovided with artillery, and the walls scarcely cannon-proof.

The three officers who most strongly opposed the withdrawal were Smith, King, and Gough. The strength of their argument lay in Smith's knowledge of the defences, for which he was responsible, he said:

> I do not hesitate to declare that I place the utmost reliance on the resources of the place, and consider them such as ought to make a good and ultimately successful defence.

Any compromise, involving the defence of the island alone, he regarded as impossible, on the ground that 'till the island is more independent in itself, there is a necessity of fairly defending the town as an outwork.' Gough satisfied himself with expressing the opinion that a withdrawal 'at the present state of forwardness of the enemy's operations' would be contrary to the spirit of Lt.-General Campbell's instructions.' It was finally decided to continue the resistance, apparently against Skerrett's desire. Part of the difficulty doubtless arose from the fact that, while Skerrett and his brigade were acting under the instructions of Cooke, the portion of the garrison under King, who came from the forces at Gibraltar, took their orders from Campbell. Cooke, influenced probably by Skerrett's reports, remained adverse to the continued occupation, while Campbell would not hear of withdrawal.

A few days passed in slight skirmishes, but, on the 29th, the French artillery succeeded not only in temporarily silencing the 16-pounder on Guzman's tower, but in effecting a breach in the wall to the right of the Portcullis tower. Skerrett now definitely decided to abandon the place and to withdraw his brigade, but King communicated the intention to Campbell, who ordered the transports to return to Gibraltar without taking a single soldier on board. Next day, the French General, Laval, sent in a summons to surrender, to which Camp Marshal Copons returned the following remarkable reply:

BATTLE OF TARIFA

When you propose to the governor of this fortress to admit a capitulation, because the breach will shortly be practicable, you certainly do not know that I am here. When the breach shall be absolutely practicable, you will find me upon it, at the head of my troops, to defend it; then we will negotiate. . . . Be pleased not to send any more flags of truce.

The Spanish boast about the defence of the breach was just as well founded as the confidence of the French in its practicability. They saw a wide breach in the wall, but they could not tell that the front of the breach was the least practicable part. Instead of leading them straight into the town, it would conduct them, should they succeed in forcing it, to a precipitous descent of fourteen feet towards a narrow street, defended on three sides, and barricaded with iron gratings, taken from the balconies of the houses. (The strength of this barricade was increased by the device of turning up every alternate bar of the gratings).

The defence of the breach was entrusted, not to Copons, but to Gough and the 87th, who flanked it from north to south. A company of the 47th under Captain Levesey, were posted on the east tower. No attack took place on the night of the 30th, but at eight o'clock next morning a general advance was made by the enemy, and about 2,000 grenadiers moved up to the breach. Gough, who had instructed his men that 'wherever there is opportunity, the bayonet must be used,' drew his sword, and ordered the band to strike up an Irish air, 'Garry-Owen.' So furious was the fire that the enemy, finding the breach less practicable than Laval had anticipated, diverted their onslaught to the Portcullis.

Here, too, Gough and the 87th were ready to receive them, and to the music of 'St. Patrick's Day' prepared to meet the advancing foe. The French could not stand the attack of the Faugh-a-Ballaghs; their leader fell outside the bars of the portcullis, close to where Gough stood in person at the head of his men; and the wounded Frenchman gave up his sword to Gough, in token of surrender. Gough received it through the bars of the portcullis. The main difficulty now was to restrain the impetuosity of the 87th. 'Colonel,' pleaded one of the regiment, as his commander forbade him to pursue, ' Colonel, I only want to tache 'em what it is to attack the aiglers.'

But not even the appeal to the glories of Barrosa could win the desired permission, and he had to be content with the hope that 'next time they come, we'll give them *Garry-Owen to glory* again.' At this point, a field-piece from the north-east tower swept the masses of the besiegers, and they were compelled to withdraw to their camp, leaving Tarifa to the possession of the gallant little band which had defended so well the honour of the British arms. Colonel Skerrett wrote in general orders issued that evening:

> On our side all behaved nobly, but the conduct of Lieut. -Col. Gough, and the 87th, whose good fortune it was to defend the breach, surpasses all praise.

Four days later, General Campbell requested Gough and the officers and men of the 87th to accept his thanks for:

> The eminent services of that distinguished corps on this day, . . .when the bravery and discipline of the 87th regiment was so conspicuously displayed in the defence of the breach.

******

Note:—In the first edition of his *History of the War in the Peninsula*, Napier gave the credit of defending the breach at Tarifa to the 47th Regiment, and referred to the 87th as occupying the portcullis tower. In the communication from which we have already quoted with reference to the battle of Barrosa, Colonel Gough drew the historian's attention to the facts that 'the whole of the east wall, in front of which the enemies' lines were, and in the centre of which was the breach, was entrusted to the 87th, from the commencement to the termination of the siege, that the 87th occupied the breach as well as the portcullis tower, which was merely a small Moorish turret, not capable of holding above twenty men and situated within ten paces of the breach.' Napier corrected the error in later editions. Gough also mentions, in the same letter, that, 'at the council of war held on the 24th Dec, most, if not all, of the officers in command of regiments and departments, gave it as their opinion that the town should not be evacuated, and subsequently recorded their opinion in writing when called on by Colonel Skerrett.'

******

Lord Proby warmly congratulated the regiment on seeing them;

> Under their truly gallant and able commander, complete the splendid military reputation they have acquired at Barrosa, by gaining fresh laurels of a description not recently worn by the

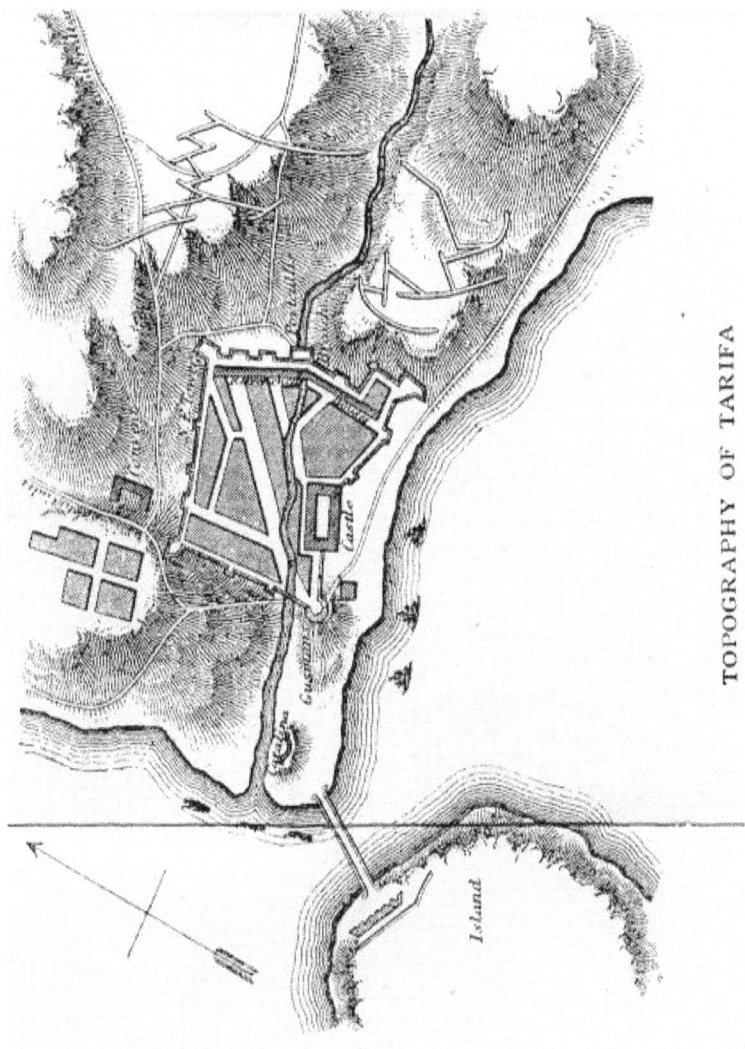

TOPOGRAPHY OF TARIFA

British Arms, by showing, in a breach opposed to the most formidable assaults, the same invincible courage with which they carried dismay into the ranks of the enemy.

Colonel Gough himself, writing to his wife four days after the assault, gave the following description of the fighting:—

Tarifa: January 4th, 1812.

My letter concluding on the second will have announced the glorious result of a storm, made by the enemy the last day of the last (to me most fortunate) year, in which your husband and his most gallant corps shone most conspicuous. How productive of fortunate events was the last year to me; I can hardly hope that this will, or indeed can, be equally so, and the conclusion, if properly stated in the despatches, will add lustre to the British arms by the conduct of our corps; not a man of any other having any share in the defence of the breach which was solely entrusted to me.

Indeed such a degree of respect are we now in, that I, in fact, command, as no one is allowed to interfere with any orders or arrangements of mine, not alone with regard to my own gallant corps, but likewise the 95th, and the detachments, together with the whole line of defence. The enemy are deserting by hundreds, and we hourly expect them to take themselves off. I will own I shall not be sorry, as everything being left to me, my mind and body are night and day on the alert.

Tarifa: January 5th, 1812.

The main body of the enemy took themselves off last night, and their rear guard this morning. I have been through all their camp and lines and batteries. This glorious result to our labours I will own was rather unexpected, the more so as Marshal Victor received positive orders from the emperor to take this place, and therefore brought with him 10,000 men and a heavy battering train of artillery, with which he has almost levelled the wall and a great part of the town. It fell to the good fortune of your husband to be appointed to the command of the whole line opposed to the enemy, all arrangements for the defences of which were solely left to him.

Therefore the breach was defended by the Prince's Own in the assault on it by 2,200 picked men covered by the fire of all their guns, and 1,200 men from the lines. The enemy were beaten with immense loss, while mine was only two killed, two sergeants two officers and eighteen men wounded—which, at least, proves that my arrangements were not bad, and on which I assure you I feel more real pride and self congratulation than on any other circumstance in my life.

Don't be frightened now when I tell you I had rather a narrow escape, which indeed in such an hour of all kinds of balls and splinters was impossible to be otherwise, a small splinter of shell having given me the merest cut in the eyebrow and a splinter of a stone rather a nasty cut in the finger. Indeed my position in the breach frequently enveloped me in mortar. I merely tell you this to prove that an all gracious power guards the life of him dear to so good a Christian. The scene was awfully grand; every officer and man seemed to outvie one another in acts of heroism, and never while life is left me can I forget their expressions and looks ... at seeing me bleed, which from exertion (being in a great heat) my temple did very freely, although at the moment and ever since I have scarcely felt I was cut.

My finger, from the cold, has festered and is annoying, which you will not be surprised at when I tell you that since the breach became practicable, now six nights back, I have never left the wall, except the night before last, when I was totally exhausted. In truth I volunteered the defence of the breach, and I could not in honour leave it as the enemy were within 270 paces of it. My boys were in a large church in the rear with their arms in their hands. Poor fellows, they never (nor did an individual) murmur, although half were always on the walls in one continued pour of rain. From the appearance of the trenches, the enemy must have been almost swimming....They have certainly buried 3 more 18-pounders and have taken off their light guns. They seem from the quantity of raw meat now about the camp to have been in no want of that article.

But as to bread, they all say they have had none for 7 days. How glorious is all this, after all our grumbling; never did British courage and discipline overcome more difficulties, a garrison of less than one thousand firelocks to drive off with disgrace ten times their numbers, from a town the walls of which were breached in 6 hours, and which is commanded from all the heights round it, in several places within 50 yards. . . . If nothing happens, I propose going home in April or May; Moore says he will come to Cadiz certainly, and accompany me. . . . We expect to go to Cadiz as soon as vessels come round for us, I own I wish it, as I am not a little knocked up, and so are my poor fellows. Indeed, I think Sir John (Doyle) should get us all to England, as we are out now over our full term of duty. From what I have said about the little scratches I have got, I only obey you in telling nothing but the truth. . . . So very trifling are they, that I would not put myself down wounded.

The valour displayed by Gough, in the defence of Tarifa, was recognised not only, as we shall see, by Wellington, but also by the Spanish authorities. There was conferred upon him the Grand Cross of the Order of Charles III of Spain, which had been instituted in 1771.

★★★★★★

Note:—There are four classes in the Order, of which the Grand Cross is the highest. The badge of the Order is a star of eight points, enamelled white, edged with gold; over the two upper points, the regal crown of Spain, chased in gold; on the centre of the star, the image of the Virgin Mary, enamelled in proper colours, vestments white and blue; on the reverse, the letters C. C. in cipher, with the number three in the centre, and this motto—*Virtuti et Merito.*

★★★★★★

At the close of the war. Colonel Gough was permitted to associate the name of Tarifa with his own, by an augmentation of his coat of arms, an honour to be described in due course.

3: The Close of the Campaign in Andalusia

From Tarifa, Gough and his victorious regiment returned to Cadiz in the end of January, being somewhat ignominiously driven into Gibraltar on the way, owing to the breaking of a cable. At Cadiz, they were received with great enthusiasm, and Gough was able to report to Doyle and Cooke upon the courage and discipline of the Prince's Own. The regiment remained at Cadiz till the end of April. It numbered at this date 730 'effective firelocks, after having lost upwards of 700 men in the country.'

Its discipline received the highest commendations from General Ross, who inspected it and gave it a report, which, says Gough, ' will do us as much good at the commander-in-chief's office as if we had gained another victory.' The report was specially welcome, as the regiment was said by hostile critics to be weak in discipline, and useful only for a wild onslaught in an hour of excitement. Its commander had also at this time the pleasure of receiving his medals for Talavera and Barrosa. In the end of March, General Cooke recognized Gough's services at Tarifa by appointing him commander of that place, and the beginning of May found him once again at 'the important fortress,' which, a year before had been 'the most wretched little village in Europe.'

At his earnest request, a large proportion of the 87th accompanied him back to the scene of their triumph. In addition to 470 of his own regiment, the garrison numbered 300 of a German battalion and 50 artillery. Tarifa was Colonel Gough's first separate command, and the fame of the recent siege gave it an added importance, and associated it still further with his name. Its proximity to Gibraltar, and its position as a British garrison in the furthest extremity of Spain, combined with the memories of the siege to make Tarifa a place which all military men visited as occasion offered. Upon the commanding officer there fell, accordingly, a considerable burden in the way of entertainment, but he was in this way brought into contact with men qualified to report to the commander-in-chief upon his capabilities as a soldier. In spite of occasional visits and still more occasional attacks, life at Tarifa proved not less tedious than at Cadiz. Gough writes:

> It is stupid to a degree, still, however, I feel glad I was appointed to the command, for it is an honourable mark of approbation. . . . I shall become quite a philosopher; this situation is quite adapted to contemplation.

Among Gough's distinguished visitors was General Cooke, and the visit had a somewhat narrow escape of acquiring an unenviable notoriety:—

> The Important Fortress of Tarifa: May 28th, 1815.
> I fear some accounts may go home on the subject of the enemies' late movements before this place. I will own I at one time expected I should have had another dust with them. Soult came to Vejer, and sent on two regiments of infantry and cavalry to within nine miles of this. I was that day out with General Cooke who came to see this place, showing him Vacinos, where the enemy most unexpectedly arrived three hours after. What a glorious kick-up it would have made had they taken the whole squad of us!
> After reconnoitring and taking all the cattle they could find, they returned to Vejer, where Marshall Soult, after treating the municipality with the utmost contempt, levied a contribution of 5,000 dollars, threatening, if not paid within two hours, he would give up the place to plunder, marched off with his booty, taking with him all his own men and leaving me in quiet possession of my government, which I trust in three months more may defy any attempt the enemy may make on it. At present I would not much have relished an attack. You may set your heart at rest on the subject of the siege of Cadiz being raised; even was it, I apprehend they would leave me quietly where I am, first as the regiments are divided, and secondly as they now see the importance of this port, almost for the salvation of Spain.
> I was most fortunate in having adopted measures which highly pleased General Cooke, and, what is rather more difficult.

General Campbell, his opponent. Nothing can get on better. I cannot avoid mentioning a circumstance that at the moment nearly gave me as much satisfaction as I ever before derived even from the conduct of my regiment in the field of battle. From the enemy's having last winter, when before this place, burned all the poor people's houses in the neighbourhood, and the present high price of bread, the lower orders of the people in this town are actually starving.

My glorious set of fellows (for which I shall ever feel truly proud of my country) sent their non-commissioned officers to me, to say if it would meet with my approval, to subscribe a day's pay per man for the relief of the poor of the town. This I declare was never even suggested by an officer to them; it was their spontaneous good feelings. Fellows like these, fighting as they have done, and feeling as they do, what is there not to be expected from them? I may abolish a Guard Room, and talk of the Cat of Nine Tails as an obsolete term.

With such men as those you may safely confide your husband, when that husband (I feel proud to say it) is almost adored by them. . . . I feel determined that no want or even wish of my soldiers, while within bounds, shall remain unsatisfied. They have better bread and meat than any soldiers even in England, I make my commissary answerable for that. They have, 'tis true, very severe duty, but they all see the necessity of it, and I am persuaded there is not a soldier who would wish to see one man less mount guard. I am also a great favourite as yet with the Spaniards. Ballesteros I have no opinion of; had I had but two of his regiments I would have taken the whole French advance the other day, while he remained looking at them, with an army that ought to have eaten them.

Take my word for it, notwithstanding all his lies, that he never will do a glorious action. He may be a good smuggler, (Ballesteros had, before the war, been employed in coastguard work), but he is no general. . . . I understand the enemy have opened again on Cadiz and the forts. You may therefore rejoice that I am not there, as every shell came over, always right over my head room, which was not bomb-proof . . . my *Casa* just happened to be in the gangway between the enemies' battery and the town. I am not a little glad you did not know this before.

The incident to which the letter refers occurred on the 13th of May, when Marshal Soult suddenly appeared at Vejer, and, leaving some sixty men outside the town, himself marched towards Tarifa and Vacinos, plundering as he went along. He demanded a ransom of 100,000 *reals*, and kept the municipal authorities imprisoned until that sum was paid. So the summer passed slowly on, with such an occasional alarm to enliven the dullness of weeks occupied with garrison duty, varied by an evening card-party or a weekly picnic under the shade of the vineyards.

The campaign of Soult in Andalusia was, by this time, nearly over. The year 1812 marks an important stage in the war. The misdeeds of the Spanish Regency had reached a crisis by the beginning of the year. The discontent of the colonies, to which reference has already been made, had passed into open rebellion, and the Spanish Government had the effrontery to employ subsidies, granted by their allies for the war in Spain, as a means of quelling the colonists. In the month of January a new Regency was proclaimed, but matters remained much the same; a new constitution followed in March, but without any real improvement in the conduct of affairs; and a considerable section of the democratic party were in favour of abandoning the struggle and making terms with Joseph. From this fate the Peninsula was delivered by the success of Wellington's operations during the year.

On January 19, fell Ciudad Rodrigo, and, on the 6th of April, Badajos, the two most important strongholds in the hands of the French on the Spanish-Portuguese frontier. Soult, who had failed to reinforce Badajos, returned to the blockade of Cadiz, and Wellington meditated an invasion of Andalusia. This design he was prevented from carrying out, as Marshal Marmont menaced the newly captured fortresses, and it was impossible for Wellington to trust their defence to the Spanish generals. The scene of the summer campaign of 1812 was, therefore, not Andalusia, but Castile, and there, on the 22nd of July, he defeated Marmont in the brilliant action of Salamanca, which laid open the way to Madrid.

Joseph became thoroughly alarmed, and sent instructions to Soult to evacuate Andalusia. These orders Soult was most unwilling to execute. The fall of Badajos, which rendered practicable a campaign of Wellington himself in Andalusia, had been a severe blow to Soult, and from the fear of such an attack he had just been relieved. He now proposed to capture Tarifa and Cadiz and to crush Ballesteros, and he had inflicted a defeat upon that general when Joseph's orders were conveyed to him. Soult urged the king to concentrate his forces in Andalusia, pointing out that the loss of Madrid was not really a matter of first importance, and dwelling upon the difficulty of a retreat. The allies had 60,000 men in Andalusia who, on Soult's retirement, would be available for pursuit, while Wellington himself was in front. Joseph's reply was a renewal of his order (although he had already deserted Madrid), and the siege of Cadiz was raised on the 25th of August. Within six weeks Soult had made good his retreat, and effected a junction with the other French troops in Valencia, whither Joseph had fled from Madrid.

Meanwhile, Wellington was engaged in an unsuccessful attempt to capture Burgos, an important French magazine in the north of Spain. The advance of Souham forced him to raise the siege, and he retreated across the Douro, pursued by Souham (October 29). Both Souham and Wellington were in expectation of reinforcements; the French general was awaiting the arrival of Joseph from Valencia, while Wellington was in daily expectation of a junction with Hill and the forces which had been detained in the south by the movements of Marshal Soult. To the march of this force it is now time to turn.

As early as August 2, Gough wrote to his wife that Soult's abandonment of Andalusia was now more than probable. On August 24 he says that four companies of the 87th had been sent to join Hill, and on September 6 he announces his resignation of the command at Tarifa, which had ceased to possess any military importance:—

Isla de Leon: 6th September, 1812.
The late occurrences make the movements of the army in Spain so uncertain, particularly that part to which I belong, that even General Cooke is quite in the dark as to what is to become of us. I gave up my command on the 31st August, and marched overland here, leaving two companies of the German battalion there. I arrived here on the 4th, and I believe shall march for Seville, where the remainder of the division are, on the 8th. I am the only corps now remaining here, except the German battalion who remain behind to take charge of the redoubts and stores. We are to remain at Seville until General Cooke receives orders from Lord Wellington; until those arrive, our future destiny is quite unsettled.
General Cooke has taken this movement on himself. I am apt to think we shall either join General Hill or Maitland; I hope

the latter. . . . The enemy has entirely evacuated this part of the country. I have been through several of their works; we were most completely deceived as to their strength. They might have been all easily carried without much loss. In coming from Tarifa, I past near Barrosa, but had not time to go over the ground, as I was commander-in-chief. I was then uncertain whether General Cooke had left this or not—he sets off tomorrow. I will own I almost regret leaving Tarifa.

Ten days later he was at Seville, and still uncertain as to future movements:—

Seville: September 15th, 1812.
We arrived at this town yesterday morning, after a very pleasant march of some days from the Isle, which town we left the day I last wrote you. . . . We that night got into Puerto Real, the principal point of defence of the French, as it covered the Trocadero. They appeared to have fortified it by surrounding it by a dry ditch with bastions. The houses of all such as fled they destroyed. As we marched for Xeres before daylight, we could hardly distinguish or make observations, but from what I could judge it is a wretched town, though rather a strong military position. On the march to Xeres on the 8th, three leagues, we past the Guadelete on which the enemy had a very strong post, and arrived at eleven o'clock at Xeres, a most beautifully situated town, in which is made all the Sherry wine sent to England.
I was billeted in the same house where Marshal Victor had his headquarters, and had the honour of sleeping in his bed. I was quite pleased with this town; it is situated on a hill and has a most extensive and beautiful view of the country, which even now is almost a vineyard. Soult, when in the lines before Cadiz, had his headquarters here, and the people seem quite Frenchified; indeed they do not conceal their sentiments. My landlord, a most gentlemanly and well informed man, was of French extraction and had the contract for provisions. He, however, was to a degree civil to me, and gave me a most excellent dinner and more real information of the French generals and their military policy than I could otherwise procure.
I went through his wine stores, supposed the largest in Europe; he has frequently shipped six thousand pipes of wine from them in one year, I was very much pleased with them, and the

cathedral, which was a very fine building. On the ninth we got to Lebrija, five leagues, and on the tenth to Los Cabas; these are two small towns without anything particular, in which the enemy generally had a few infantry and cavalry to keep up the communications on the Seville road on which they are. On the 11th we got to Utrera, where we met the Guards and the heavy brigade of nine-pounders. This, though not very large, is considered one of the richest towns in the south of Spain; some of the houses are magnificent.

On the 12th we reached Dos Hermanas (two sisters) a small village, and yesterday arrived in this quarter. The road from Isla here is to a degree beautiful, however it wants water. The people, particularly in the last village (we having been the first red coats they ever saw) were to a degree civil and seemed delighted, with the exception of Puerto Real and Xeres. This is a very magnificent city, formerly the capital of Spain. The public buildings are superb to a degree. The cathedral far surpasses anything I ever saw, but I have been so much hurried with regimental duties that I have had very little time for observation. I was at the theatre last night and was much pleased, the performers seemed better than those at Cadiz, except the dancers, but the house is not near so good, about the size of the Hay Market, but far more beautiful.

The streets, however, are uncommonly narrow and not at all clean, the houses are very irregular. The town appears twice the size of Cadiz. The Almeida, or public walk, the Spaniards call one of the wonders of the world; it runs several miles along the River Guadalquivre, which is a beautiful river and navigable up to the town for small vessels. It is to me the most extraordinary thing that ever occurred, how the enemy could have been so deceived, as the allies had to cross the bridge, which is a very strong position and the city is walled. They had between three and four thousand infantry and two regiments of cavalry in town. We had now 1,600 British and six thousand Spaniards, which one thousand French would have drove before them.

They knew Skerret was in their neighbourhood and his force, and had no idea of his daring to attack them. They were all at breakfast when they heard that a host of red coats were pouring down the hills close to the town, our advance were certainly in the suburbs when their general was (*word here illegible*). They therefore thought it was General Hill and fled in the most disgraceful confusion, their officers, such as collected in the hurry, could not get the men to stand against the red coats. The conduct of the inhabitants was enthusiastic, long before the enemy left the town the joy bells in all the churches began ringing, and the stragglers were pelted by the people, who ran out and embraced our men; several cheering on the English were actually wounded in the batteries. Villatte was to have retired in two days after, before which he was to have raised a contribution that was tantamount to sacking the town, after which the division that retired from the lines was to have come in and given it the finishing stroke.

Well therefore might the inhabitants have rejoiced. When I see more of the public buildings, I will give you, or rather will attempt to give you, some description of them. . . . General Cooke waits for orders; some say we are to spend the winter here, I think not. We have not a Frenchman within 130 miles of us. Cooke is here, I dine with him today; he is still as attentive as ever to me. We are in Lord Proby's brigade, who is not a little proud of us—however, I have found the detachment in shocking order, but am making every exertion to fit them out. I have upwards of seven hundred with me.

The movement in which Cooke's force was engaged was designed to harass Soult's retreat, or, rather to reinforce Sir Rowland Hill. But Soult was already far on his road to Valencia, and Cooke hurried forward to join Hill, with a view to a concentration with the commander-in-chief, now engaged in the siege of Burgos. They marched through a desolate and devastated country to Truxillo, which they reached on October 14. This advance involved some severe marching, and Gough rejoices in the reputation which his regiment was achieving:—

Truxillo: Oct 14th, 1812.
We have got thus far on our route to join General Hill, who is either at Toledo or Aranjuez. This town is quite destroyed, I really would not know it: my old billet is in ruins. I regret to tell you the weather has, I fear, set in for the first rains, which generally last a fortnight, which will about bring us to the end of our march. My men have astonished the division in marching; I never saw such a set of fellows. I came yesterday seven

and twenty miles over a most wretched road, and it raining all the time, in eight hours and a half, without having one man out of his section an inch. The Guards saw us come in to their astonishment. Skerrett, who was present, cried out 'G—d—n me, my brigade, let them look at that regiment, and be ashamed of themselves.' I trust the fellows will continue, if they do there will be nothing but comfort. . . . The day after tomorrow we shall cross the Tagus at Almaraz, where we shall see the scene of Sir R. Hill's last brilliant affair. ... It is here reported that Marquis Wellington has taken Burgos and that one or two of his divisions are on their march to join Sir R. Hill: if so, I have some hopes still of seeing William, which I own I should be very glad of.

At this point there is a break in Gough's correspondence. His regiment continued its march to join Hill at Aranjuez, and reached him in time to take part in the defence of the Puente Larga, a bridge near the junction of the Jarama with the Henares, and to accompany the retreat from Madrid to Salamanca, to join the commander-in-chief. It is, for our purpose, unnecessary to describe the incidents of the next fortnight, in which neither Wellington's nor Soult's intentions are absolutely clear. On the 15th of October, Wellington, having failed to bring about a pitched battle, continued his retreat, and the army went into winter quarters. The general position selected by Wellington for this purpose, extended from Plasencia and Coria to Lamego, in Portugal. The 87th was separated from the 4th Division with which it had acted since joining Hill, and rejoined the 2nd Brigade of the 3rd Division, stationed in Portugal.

Gough writes from near Lamego in December, but the letters which follow speak of changes, and we find him, consecutively, at Villa de Ponte, at Adbarros, at Quinta de Robira, and finally, in April, at Vide. The retreat from Burgos and Madrid was an inglorious ending to a year of triumph, and the British Army was disheartened to the last degree. As a natural consequence, its discipline deteriorated. The men plundered and mutinied, and, at the small combat of the Huebra, at the beginning of the retreat, some of the general officers deliberately ignored the orders of the commander-in-chief, and, but for Wellington's promptness, might have caused a heavy disaster. All through the winter, complaints continue about the condition of the army, and Gough attributes the discontent partly to disappointment and ill-health, and partly to the disgraceful outbursts which had followed the capture of Ciudad Rodrigo and Badajos. The general discontent had infected the 87th, and Gough's letters are full of illustrations of the difficulties of that dreadful winter. The buoyant tone of his letters changes at the end of November, when he describes:

> The miseries of a retreat in winter, and the feelings of an officer, commanding, not a fortnight back, one of the nicest corps in the service, now reduced to half its numbers, and that half broken-spirited and starved.

A fortnight later, he gives a more detailed account of his troubles:—

> Fort Alcada (five leagues from Lamego): Dec, 9th, 1812.
> ...We have at length got into what is called Winter Quarters, in a most wretched little village, but I trust as we are very crowded, with the 94th Regt. we shall get removed to some other quarters—as nothing can be worse than this. ... The battalion is so cut up from its late march, that it quite sickens me to look at them, particularly as the means of getting them shortly again into order is not within my reach—I mean money, necessaries, &c. ... This battalion having been paid at Seville to 24th Oct., while the army here have only been paid to 24th July, they now, when it is required, get two months' pay; we get nothing.
> When I reflect on what we were, when we left Seville, and what we are, I will own I have scarcely heart to undertake a total equipment and reorganization of the battalion. There are difficulties attending on 2nd Battalions which scarcely can be surmounted on service, and Col. Fulton, from the class of men he sent us, has done the battalion more injury than any other officer can ever repair. They will ever distinguish themselves in the field, but I fear it will be a long time before they can bear a review. Want of provisions has also produced thieving, which is hard to eradicate, I am sorry to say, in an Irishman.

The numbers of the corps continued to decrease: in the beginning of January it was only 350 strong; a month later, out of 400 men, 65 were in hospital.

> The army at large are in a very shocking way, several corps not more than my strength have two hundred in hospital—I mean Regimental Hospital, the General Hospitals are full.

The morale of the 87th continued good, and the men showed an attachment to their corps and to their commander which was very gratifying to Gough's feelings. An unfortunate incident occurred in March; the misconduct of a few men, while bringing military stores from Lisbon, brought upon the 87th a severe and largely unmerited censure from Wellington. It is probable that Wellington wished to make an example, for insubordination was so common that, as Gough remarks, 'Courts-martial are the order of the day throughout the army.' The incident is noteworthy only as it contributed to give a general impression of want of discipline in the 87th—a charge which Gough repudiates by reference to the reports of Generals Graham and Cooke, and the other officers under whom it had served.

4: Vittoria and Nivelle

Wellington spent the winter months in making preparations for the campaign of Vittoria. Reinforcements reached him from England, and it is estimated that in the spring of 1813 he had nearly 200,000 troops (British, Spanish, and Portuguese) under his command. He had been, in the preceding September, appointed Commander-in-Chief of the Spanish armies, and, in January, he paid a visit to Cadiz to lay his plans before the Cortes. While the campaign of 1813 opened with an increase of the numbers under Wellington's control, the forces of the enemy had been diminished owing to the mortality of the Russian campaign, but they still remained about 30,000 in excess of the allied armies. The French were in four divisions; in the north, they held the Tormes and the Esla; in the north-west, Cafarelli separated the British from their fleet in the Bay of Biscay; while, in the south, one division held the Tagus, and another covered Madrid.

In these circumstances, Wellington determined to strike a blow before they were ready, and to evade the defences of the Tormes and the Douro by turning the right flank of the enemy. This important movement he entrusted to General Graham, the hero of Barrosa. Early in May the scheme was arranged, and Graham was instructed to cross the Douro, march through the Tras-os-Montes to Zamora, and thence northwards to Valladolid. Graham's force included the 3rd Division now under Picton. Gough writes on May 14 in good spirits; they are on the point of departure, his men are in excellent order and spirits, and the rank and file now numbers 510. We have no further account of his march; but it can have been no easy task to make their way through that wild country.

While Graham was traversing the Tras-os-Montes, Wellington forced back the French from the line of the Tormes, and reached a point between Miranda de Duero and Toro. Graham's appearance on the right bank of the Esla took the French by surprise, and they retreated first to Zamora and then to Toro, whence the concentration of Wellington's army drove them still backwards. From Toro Wellington advanced to Valladolid, in pursuit not only of the army which had held the line of the Douro, but also of the army of the south, under Joseph, which, fearing that it might be cut off, was marching with all haste to join the army of Portugal. Had this concentration taken place earlier, Wellington's task in such a country, and against so large a number of the enemy, would have been something very different from the triumphal march which Gough describes in a letter written early in June:—

Camp (two leagues in front of Palencia): June 8th (1813). . . . We got into Palencia the day before yesterday at three o'clock. The intrusive king reviewed the French troops the day previous, and left the town at five in the evening, after which they commenced their retreat taking all they could carry off. Their cavalry left the town six hours before we came in. Notwithstanding, you would imagine we were at peace. I go as regularly to bed in sheets as I would in England and with as little prospect of being disturbed. I own it is quite a new thing to me. . . . Lord Wellington, in passing the brigade the other day, on the march, pulled in his horse in rear of the regiment, on which he kept his eyes so steadfastly fixed during the quarter of an hour he remained in their rear, and the whole time he took walking his horse along their flank.
I never saw so minute an inspection. When he got to our head he again put spurs to his horse and galloped on. We were marching in prime order; he said not a word. It is said the Enemy are destroying the works of Burgos and are determined to retire behind the Ebro, so I fear there will be little chance for some length of time for us to distinguish ourselves.

The rumour about Burgos, improbable as it seemed, turned out to be correct. The French had trusted to keeping back the enemy at the Douro, and had left the new fortifications of Burgos unfinished, but sufficiently high to command the older defences which resisted the besiegers in the preceding year. The fortress which had put a limit to Wellington's victorious career after Salamanca, fell, therefore, into his hands without a struggle, and the French continued their retreat to the Ebro. It was decided to hold this strongly, and a detachment was left to guard the left flank at Pancorbo, while the line of the river was occupied down to Haro, Wellington adopted precisely the same device that had served him so well at the crossing of the Douro, except that he now turned the French position with his whole army, instead of with one division. Graham's experience among the Tras-os-Montes showed the possibility of leading an army and of moving artillery through mountainous country, and Wellington decided to cross the upper waters of the Ebro, and to repeat Graham's exploit by marching through the mountains on the borders of Guipuzcoa. On June 18, Gough wrote to his wife, relating some of the incidents of their rapid march.

> We crossed the Ebro at St. Martin, on the 15th, and have been making long and distressing marches since, through the boldest, most mountainous, and romantic country I ever beheld. The Spaniards deserve to lose their country for not having defended the passes of the Ebro, and indeed, all the country to the north of it. I was much disappointed on finding that river, this far up, quite a stream. The inhabitants either dislike or fear us much, as they have forsaken most of the villages we have past through. We have latterly been badly off for bread, but our General (Picton) has been indefatigable in his exertions. The Seventh Division have been with us for some days. I have therefore seen a good deal of William, who is quite well. . . . I am happy to tell you my men are getting on capitally—only eight sick, after all my fatigues. The whole army are in high order and spirits.

The feeling of confidence seems to have been general, Gough says:

> I am sanguine that this will be the most brilliant campaign for the Grand Lord that he has ever attempted.

On the 19th of June, Wellington was encamped on the Bayas, facing the French position at Vittoria. It is not necessary, in a biography of Lord Gough, to do more than give the merest outline of the famous action that followed on the 21st. The French position was chosen with that lack of military insight which characterized all the movements of the well-meaning Joseph. The River Zadora turns almost at right angles in front of Vittoria, and the French were drawn up along the river bank, presenting a double face to the attack of the allies, and covered by a stream crossed by seven bridges which they did not attempt to hold. The centre and left stretched from the village of Hermandad to the heights of Puebla, while the right (the army of Portugal) was seven

miles distant. Wellington divided his army into three columns and arranged a simultaneous attack upon the French. Sir Thomas Graham
was entrusted with the assault upon the right wing of the enemy, and
Sir Rowland Hill with the assault on their left, while the commander-
in-chief took charge of the centre. In spite of some scarcely avoidable
delay, these movements were effectually carried out, and Graham and
Hill soon menaced the enemy's flanks. Gough, with the rest of the 3rd
Division under Picton, formed part of Wellington's left centre, and
reached the field somewhat late.

Along with the 7th Division, under Lord Dalhousie, they took a
distinguished part in the action, and Gough, with the 87th, made a
brilliant charge, and captured the village of Hermandad. The French
centre began to give way, and soon were in full retreat, pursued by
Picton and Dalhousie, towards Vittoria. Earlier in the day Hill had carried La Puebla, and the gallant stand made by Reille and the army of
Portugal against Graham was rendered useless by the retreat of Joseph
and the centre, which exposed their left and rear. Reille therefore
withdrew his forces and succeeded in keeping them in good order, so
long as they were separated from the frightened rout of the French
centre.

This of course could not be for long, and the whole French Army
was soon in helpless and hopeless flight. In the following letter Gough
describes the fight, and refers to the enormous amount of spoil which
was one of the features of the victory. He was himself unwounded,
although he had been hit in three places: 'the skin,' he says, 'not broken.' A shot had passed through his coat in two or three places, and his
horse had been killed under him, he says:

> The officers are surprised I brought my men under such a tre-
> mendous fire; they would be more astonished if they had been
> in it.

> Camp (before Vittoria): June 22nd, 1813.
> My beloved will rejoice to hear that the opportunity of distin-
> guishing myself and the Corps occurred yesterday, the glorious
> twenty-first June. The battalion out-Heroded Herod, its con-
> duct called forth the warmest encomiums from General Col-
> ville, who witnessed a part of its conduct. After the action he
> said before several officers, 'Gough, you and your corps have
> done wonders.' But, by the bye, he did not see all, a village hav-
> ing separated me from the rest of the brigade, when I charged

two heights on which were a numerous force of artillery, supported by a heavy column of Infantry, I should think about two thousand, without a corps to assist us. My good fortune still supports me, as I found one of my sergeants got the *batonner* (truncheon) of Marshal Jourdan, who commanded the French, carried, I should think by one of his staff who was killed. I shall present it tomorrow to General Colville for Lord Wellington. Unfortunately no officer saw the fellow take it, I should therefore fear our action will not appear. . . . It is a staff about two feet long covered with purple velvet, most beautifully embroidered with eagles. The young rascal has taken off the two gold eagles on either end, which he pretends he has lost. I cannot express to you my satisfaction at the conduct of the officers and men, they really have proved themselves heroes, which indeed I understand have all the other corps of this division. We have taken innumerable guns, I should think nearly the whole the enemy had, and the whole of their baggage. Some of my fellows have made fortunes, but much less than the old soldiers of other corps. I passed some hundred carriages, some beautiful, all laden with trunks &c. I hear, full of gold. I have purchased some plate and a magnificent sword. I regret to tell you my loss was enormous, but few when I reflect on the tremendous fire we were in for two hours and a half.

The *bâton* was presented by Wellington to the prince regent who sent him, in return, that of a field-marshal of the British Army.

The plunder of Vittoria had its usual sequel in the degeneration of discipline, which prevented the allies from using to the full the opportunities afforded by the complete rout of Joseph's army, and, while Wellington began the sieges of Pampeluna and San Sebastian, the Emperor sent Soult to reorganise the wreck of the armies in Spain. Only one army remained in the east of Spain, and the British force under Sir John Murray should have kept a check upon it and its commander, Suchet. Murray, however, embarked his men, and Wellington's movements were now threatened by the possibility of an advance by Suchet. He therefore undertook only the siege of San Sebastian which he could not leave in his rear, and blockaded Pampeluna. Gough and the 87th were in the latter portion of the army; on June 30 he writes from halfway between Pampeluna and Saragossa, engaged in an attempt to cut off General Clausel from France; the attempt was unsuccessful, and on July 16 he is again in the north, occupied with the blockade of Pampeluna.

His regiment has behaved well, and he boasts that only two of the 87th have fallen out, while from fifty to a hundred of all other corps have dropped by the way. Soult had now taken command, and on the 24th he advanced to the relief of San Sebastian and Pampeluna. The immediate result was the first check to the British arms since the retreat from Burgos. Soult succeeded in driving out the enemy from the passes of Maya and Roncesvalles, and Cole and Picton, who had been in command at Roncesvalles, retreated to Huarte. Gough does not describe this retreat in any extant letter, and, when he next writes, a week later, the situation had been retrieved by Wellington himself. Returning rapidly from San Sebastian, when he understood the danger arising from Soult's appearance, he surprised Picton's force by his sudden arrival, and possibly restrained Soult from making an immediate attack. In the two battles of Sorauren, fought on July 28 and 30, Soult was completely defeated, and driven back over the frontier into France. In these the 87th had no share of the fighting, but Gough's account of the action is interesting:—

> Camp (one mile above the clouds): August 2nd, 1813. We ascended yesterday from Roncesvalles (the celebrated) to our present exalted situation, which, though much nearer Heaven, partakes nothing of what we paint to ourselves are the pleasures and comforts experienced there. Except bilberries is the food of the Inhabitants, I know of no other they can possibly procure in this wretched region, and playing hide and go seek in the clouds—I know of no other possible pastime. In short, we are encamped on a heath on the summit of the Pyrenees, and in a thick mist, but for which we could see many leagues into France, from which we are about six or eight miles—our object to cover the pass of Roncesvalles, which we passed through in our ascent, but which is commanded by this mountain.
> From the pass, which is below the cloud, we had a most extended view of France, which appeared just under us, and was very inviting. The little town of Roncesvalles, which is at the Spanish side of the mountain, just under the pass, and is the most beautiful and romantic situate place you can paint to your imagination, I quite regretted leaving it. The Pyrenees are near-

ly wooded to their summit with very fine beech, and are very grand indeed. This pass is that which Soult came lately through and which the Fourth Division abandoned, just as we came up to them; both divisions then fell back to Huarte, the village we formerly were quartered in, close to Pampeluna, where Sir Thomas Picton took up a position, placing us, his own division, on the right of the village, which he conceived the most assailable, the Fourth Division on the left, supported by a brigade of the 2nd and the Spaniards.

The enemy pressed close after us, and we scarcely had got into position when their Columns made their appearance, but unfortunately (perhaps you will think otherways) for us, they attacked the hills on which the Fourth Division were posted, leaving 7,000 Infantry and 2,500 cavalry in front of us, so close that Colonel Duglas' guns frequently fired over them—a small rivulet only separated us. We every moment expected them, but that was not Soult's intention. . . . During the night, the enemy moved columns to his right, for the purpose of turning our left, which he would have done but for the providential arrival of the 6th division at the very critical moment. These attacks were very formidable as to numbers, but as to spirit miserable. This day they again attacked the hill twice, and were twice repulsed at the point of the bayonet.

Conceive how interesting this was to us, who could see every part of it and close to us. It was quite a show. Early the third morning, the *marquis* came up to our hill. I was standing with Thos. Picton, who with Sir Stapleton Cotton, Generals Colville and Ponsonby, was with us the whole time. He appeared in the most wonderful good spirits, and shook Sir Thos. (who by the bye he has not been hitherto on good terms with) most heartily by the hand. It was this day supposed that Soult, finding himself foiled on the left, would have attacked the right. We were therefore all prepared, but alas no such thing. . . . The night passing, at daylight we saw the enemy in full retreat, but supposing it to be manoeuvring we did not follow till 10 o'clock.

Our division then pushed forward, and we were in hopes we should have made up for lost time. He kept on the hills, and we were on the main road just below him, on his flank . . . we did not bring him into action, although for two leagues we were within half a mile of his columns. I will own I felt much disappointed as I think our division might have done much more, had they either pushed in (as they latterly did) and got in the enemy's rear, or ascended the hill and attacked his flank. We however made him alter his point of retreat. The whole business was grand to a degree and glorious. It is estimated that the enemy's loss has been at least 15,000. He brought 45,000 into the country, and there are nine thousand still straggling amongst these mountains.

The fighting division, (the local nickname of the 3rd), or the 3rd consisted of 3 companies of the 60th, 5th, 45th, 74th, 83rd, 87th, 88th, and 94th Btns., 9th and 21st Portuguese. We were for the first time without fighting and all disappointed, except the 45th and 74th, . . . Lord Wellington is certainly a very great, but he is a very fortunate man. He has now fully crippled the enemy, who, between ourselves, had they not made some blunders, and had fought like men, would have crippled him. The French peasantry are all in arms, and frightened at our being so near neighbours. Was it left with me, I would at once move into France. It is expected that the garrison of Pampeluna finding Soult's failure, surrendered the day we left it. If they have not, they shortly must for want of provisions. St Sebastian must also very shortly follow. What they will do with us then God knows.

Soult's retreat into France cut off Suchet from any possible co-operation with the rest of the French army, and the arrival of Lord William Bentinck to replace Murray freed Wellington from any danger from the only French Army left in Spain. The Maya Pass and the Pass of Roncesvalles were again held by the British forces, while the siege of San Sebastian was renewed with vigour. Gough was stationed in the Maya Pass, whence he writes on August 12:—

We have been in this pass two days, together with the 6th Division (now under the command of General Colville). I thought the scenery of Roncesvalles grand, but this is infinitely superior. From our camp we see from twenty to thirty leagues into France, studded with towns and villages, with a most extensive view of the Bay of Biscay. . . . We look over on the French camp, in which it appears they have very few men. It is said they have marched some heavy columns to the right (their left). I own I do not think Soult will, from the loss of one action, give up a kingdom. I am persuaded he will again try to raise the siege of

Pamplona, by pushing through the Maya Pass (to the right of Roncesvalles), shewing columns at the same time on our right to keep us here, while Suchet threatens the right, and perhaps joins him.

To counterbalance this 50,000 Spaniards join us, 5,000 British from England, 2,000 Guards from Oporto, and about the same number of the slight cases from Vittoria and Pamplona. This will enable His Lordship again to set you English all agog . . . and I own I think the time fast approaches. But don't be uneasy, if I thought there was any chance of this battalion being much employed, I should not have been so very communicative. . . . Tell Edward, (his son), he must not be frightened, that the French will not eat his papa until he gets fatter, which there does not appear much chance of, in these mountains.

Eight days later, his estimate of Soult's intentions has changed.

We are still in the Maya Pass, the enemy in our front are very weak in numbers, but in position very favourable. They say they hourly expect to hear of a general peace; under this conviction they do not even fire on some of our light troops, who have struggled into France to collect vegetables.

Meanwhile, San Sebastian and Pamplona were still holding out; the former fell on August 31, and the latter exactly two months later. During this time, Soult remained on the defensive, holding the line from Ainhoue to the coast, while Suchet was detained by Bentinck in Catalonia. Gough's division continued to garrison the Maya Pass, and two months elapsed before he was again in action. The time passed quietly, with an occasional excursion into the mountains, a rumour that they were to be sent into Catalonia, and the excitement of the arrival of dispatches. These, indeed, can have brought little satisfaction to the 87th, whose services at Vittoria received scant recognition. Wellington had just made a rule not to name in dispatches regimental commanding officers, except those who had been killed, as he found that the opposite practice was productive of never-ending jealousies.

It may be doubted if the decision was a wise one, and it must have been somewhat disheartening to the colonel of the 87th, for alike at Barrosa, at Tarifa, and even at Vittoria, circumstances had made Gough, for the time, his own commanding officer. He had now commanded a battalion longer than probably any other officer in the Peninsula; the only French *bâton* and the first French eagle captured in the war had fallen to the 87th, and Wellington himself had declared that their courage at Tarifa was greater than could reasonably be expected even of British soldiers. The disappointment of the dispatches was, however, amply atoned for a few weeks later, when Wellington himself gave to Gough a 'full and most gratifying explanation' and an invitation to memorialise, through the commander-in-chief, for a medal for Talavera.

While Wellington was preparing for the attack upon Soult, and an action was imminent, Gough's thoughts were distracted by the news of the death of his little son, Edward, whom he had not seen since his birth, but of whom his home letters had been full. (The child had been born on December 9, 1810, during a second visit home paid by Colonel Gough in the course of that year). His letter of consolation to his wife was written on the 3rd of November; a week later his attention was once more diverted by the approach of another important action, his last, as it turned out, in the Peninsular War.

In the Battle of the Nivelle (November 9, 1813), Gough and the 87th bore an honourable part. The French line of defence stretched across twelve miles, and the fighting on both sides took place in three divisions. On the British right Hill was opposed to d'Erlon, in the centre Beresford faced Clausel, and Hope commanded our left wing against Reille. In the morning, the British carried all three positions, and drove the French upon their second line of defence. The moral effect of this early repulse was very great, and Soult's army was further depressed by the news (unknown to the Allies) that Napoleon had suffered his great defeat at Leipsic.

The British had entered on the struggle full of confidence, and Wellington's admirable strategy was carried out as he wished. By nightfall, the French position ('strong by nature,' says Gough, 'and made as strong as art can make it') was in the hands of the enemy. The 87th, under Colville, had been stationed on the right of the British centre, close to Zugaramundi, with the rest of the 3rd Division. The division was given a part in the heavy fighting which took place round the village of Sarre, in front of which the French had constructed two formidable redoubts, and later in the day they were sent against the fortifications of Saint Pé. In one of these actions (it is not clear which) Gough was wounded. In a note written to his wife the same evening, he says:—

Don't be frightened, my darling Frances, by seeing your old

man's name in the list of wounded. I got a hard rap in the hip, but the bone is not touched. I however fear it will be some time before I will be well. However, I fully did, I trust, my duty—one comfort, I feel I did. I fear I lost most severely—three other officers wounded are in the room with me.

The 87th had fully maintained its reputation, he says:

The old corps behaved as usual. . . . Nothing could withstand the Prince's Own. Old Colville cried out, 'Royal 87th, Glorious 87th,' and well he might.

Gough had been removed to hospital at Zugaramundi where he remained till the end of the year. His letters to his wife report gradual progress; by the beginning of December he is able to go about on crutches, on Christmas Day he entertains a party of wounded friends to celebrate the arrival of Colville's dispatch on the battle, one sentence of which runs:—

The major-general is happy to communicate the latest information received from the medical officers in the rear, that the severe wound of Lt. Colonel Gough of the 87th, does not threaten more than the temporary loss of his very valuable services.

It was, of course, a great disappointment to be unable to take his part in the victory of the Nive and Saint Pierre, although it brought some comfort that the 87th, not being engaged, had not entered the field under any other commander. His wound progressed slowly. A removal, on a bullock conveyance, to a new hospital at Restoria did not help his convalescence, and he saw none of the little fighting that remained for the Peninsular forces. Wellington remained in winter quarters till the middle of February; on the 27th, he won the Battle of Orthes, and, a fortnight afterwards, Beresford entered Bordeaux. Soult made some further resistance, but the abdication of the Emperor Napoleon put an end to the long struggle.

Gough writes his last Peninsular letter from hospital at Restoria, on February 28th—he hopes to be home in a month. Of the precise date of his arrival and of the long hoped for meeting there is no record. Among all the wanderings in many climes which lay before him in the future, there was not to be another visit to Spain. Long years afterwards, when he had attained almost the highest honours for which a British soldier may wish, he spent some months, in hale and vigorous old age, at Saint Jean de Luz. One day he disappeared, taking with him a small grandson, (later Colonel Hugh Grant, C.B., who commanded, from 1891 to 1895, the regiment in which his grandfather had served in the West Indies—the 78th or Seaforth Highlanders). His family and the little community, who took a pride in their distinguished visitor, became alarmed and were going out to search for him, when he appeared tired and hatless, he said:

> If I have not been again in Spain, at all events, my hat is there, for it blew off at the top of the hill, as I looked down upon the soil of the Peninsula.

Nearly six years of strenuous work lay 'over the hills and far away,' in the treasure-house of memories which few living men could share with him. He had laid there the foundations of fame and fortune, and he had been the almost idolized leader of a gallant and devoted battalion. His commanding officers, and the great duke himself, had expressed the highest appreciation of the achievements of the 87th and their colonel. Wellington wrote to Sir John Doyle, in the summer of 1814:

> I should be very ungrateful if I was not ready to apply for promotion for the gallant officers who have served under my command, and will forward Colonel Gough's Memorial.

Recollections of the Peninsula remained a permanent possession and had their influence upon his future career. He had seen the strategy of Wellington at Talavera; he had taken his share in the brilliant campaign of Vittoria, when the difficulties of a dangerous and delicate position vanished before the military genius of his commander; he had witnessed the sudden and dramatic appearance of the chief as the two armies faced each other on the Pyrenees, and he had borne his part in the almost faultless carrying out of the attack upon the extended front along the Nivelle. The lessons thus learned bore fruit in China, and in India, where Wellington's own early reputation had been won.

Rewards of a substantial kind were freely bestowed by a grateful country upon the soldiers of the Peninsula. In August, Gough was awarded a pension of £250 a year, increased in 1816 to £300. The medal for Talavera, for which Wellington had applied, was duly granted, and the Brevet-Rank of Lieutenant-Colonel was, on the duke's representation, antedated to the date of his Talavera Dispatches. In 1815, the prince regent conferred upon him the honour of Knighthood, and he was permitted to adopt the following augmentation of his coat of arms—

> In chief, a representation of the fortress of Tarifa, with the Cross of the Order of Charles III pendent; and as an additional crest, An arm vested in the uniform of the 87th Regiment, supporting a banner inscribed with the number of the regiment, and grasping at the same time a French Eagle reversed, in commemoration of the one taken by that corps at Barrosa.

Colonel Gough's correspondence from the Peninsula throws considerable light upon the character of the writer. It is impossible to peruse these letters without being deeply impressed with the sincerity and earnestness of purpose of the soldier who penned them, with his devotion to his profession, his loyalty to those in authority over him, his regard for the happiness of those committed to his charge, and with the soldierly instinct which led his battalion to victory on so many well-fought fields. But the impression left is not only that of a gallant and humane soldier.

Gough's deep religious spirit, his trust in an all-wise Providence which he believed to have him in special protection, and his honourable and unswerving acceptance of all that he judged to be the direction of Providence, are features that marked his younger days in Spain not less than his later campaigns in India. His affection for the faith in which he had been nurtured and for the Church of which he was a member was unwavering. But, while he accepted loyally the principles of the Church of Ireland, he was unusually liberal in his attitude towards the religion of the majority of his fellow countrymen. His letters breathe a love for Ireland and an interest in her welfare, and he regarded the religious disabilities as a great menace to a proper understanding between the two countries. He writes in June, 1812:

> I wish to God, the prince had declared for Catholic Emancipation. This measure in the end he must give way to, and every hour injures his popularity.

The letters show also the warmth of the writer's family affection. He had two brothers serving in the Peninsular Army—Captain George Gough of the 28th Regiment, and Major William Gough of the 68th, who distinguished himself at Salamanca, and to whom there are various references in his brother's letters. Of them, of his father, and of other members of his own family he often speaks, and

115

his devoted affection to his wife and children is a frequent theme of these numerous letters. Such expressions of affection he would not himself have regarded as fit matter for the printed page, and they have been omitted from the letters we have quoted. So powerful, however, were these emotions that his letters record a not infrequent conflict between them and the desire for military-glory and the love of serving his country.

Through a large part of his later life, the separation from his wife, which was the cause of this conflict, was avoided by the courage of Lady Gough, who accompanied him to India, and whose presence was, to a man of his temperament, a source of inspiration and strength. While in garrison at Tarifa and at Cadiz, he made plans for her arrival in Spain, but the nature of the operations in which the army was engaged prevented their execution, and he could receive only letters and such parcels of provisions as it was possible to send. To Cadiz and Tarifa there came from England a succession of hampers which relieved Colonel Gough from many of even the lesser privations of a state of siege, and as long as he was stationed there, there was a reasonable probability of such things reaching him. References to lump sugar and fish sauce read curiously in the circumstances of a beleaguered town and remind one how complete was the British command of the sea.

Throughout almost the whole of the war, Gough's health continued excellent, except for his attack of fever in June, 1809, and for some inconveniences resulting from the wound he received at Talavera. In January, 1813, in the course of his wanderings while the army was in winter quarters before the campaign of Vittoria, he writes—

> Do not, I pray you, entertain so erroneous an opinion as that my constitution is broken; 'tis true I am not as strong as I was, but there are very few in this army more capable of undergoing fatigue. When I tell you I never sit down from breakfast to dinner-hour, except to write a letter, you will see my health must be good. I have not had a cold this winter, although I have no fireplace in my room, and there is not a day that I am not wet in my feet, often all over.

This confidence in his own powers of physical endurance continued to be characteristic of him throughout the whole of his life, and it was fully justified by the event. In India, in China, and at home, during the long period of rest and retirement which he was destined to enjoy, his constitution remained sound and his frame vigorous, and this active and strenuous habit of body must receive due weight in any appreciation of his military career.

5: Public Life

It is one of the difficulties of the biographer of a soldier that the events which it is his duty to relate are crowded into a few years of what may be a long life. Five years in Spain, two in China, and five in India comprise that period of Sir Hugh Gough's nine decades of life in which alone he was enabled to give to his country the services which have rendered his name illustrious, and which entitle him to a place and a memorial among British soldiers. When he sailed for Cadiz, to serve under Wellington in the Peninsula, he was under thirty years of age; when he landed in China, to take command of the Expeditionary Force, he was over sixty. The years which intervened between the Battle of the Nivelle in 1813 and the assault upon Canton in 1841 were not all spent in retirement.

The work of Sir Hugh Gough during this period was worthy to be done and it was done worthily; nor can there be any doubt that it helped to train and to fit him for high and responsible duties in the days to come. But it passed away and left little or no record; even if record there were, it would claim but slight space in this book.

The 2nd Battalion of the 87th Regiment had continued to distinguish itself in the Peninsular War, even after Colonel Gough's wound had rendered him incapable of leading it into the field. It was engaged in several skirmishes with the French; it behaved with distinction, and it suffered heavily, in the action at Orthes on February 27, 1814; and it shared in the victory of Toulouse. On the abdication of Napoleon, the Peninsular Army was broken up, and the battalion marched from Toulouse to Pouillac, and disembarked at Cork in the end of July. After a month spent in Ireland, it went into garrison at Plymouth, where it remained till December, 1814. The American War of 1812-14 was still in progress, and, for a month, the battalion guarded the prisoners at Dartmoor. In the end of the year, it was transferred to its old quarters at Guernsey, where its Colonel, Sir John Doyle, was Governor. It remained at Guernsey during the memorable year 1815, and had no share in the glories of Waterloo. On recovering from his wound, Sir Hugh Gough had again taken command, and, on May 25, 1815, he was gazetted Lieutenant-Colonel, having held that brevet rank for six years.

★★★★★★

Note:—The recovery was slow and tedious. On June 24, 1814, he writes: 'I am still on crutches, when I am able to leave my bed, which is not often the case, as my health, exclusive of the wound, has suffered severely.'

★★★★★★

After the European settlement which followed Napoleon s imprisonment in St. Helena, there was a natural desire to reduce the army establishment, the burden of which had pressed heavily on the nation during twenty years of warfare. Among the corps which it became necessary to sacrifice to the desire for economy, was the 2nd Battalion of the 87th. It had been removed from Guernsey in April, 1816, first to Portsmouth, and then to Colchester, and it was from Colchester Barracks, on January 24, 1817, that Colonel Gough issued his regimental orders on the disbandment of the corps. He said, after a recital of the deeds of the battalion:

> The Princes Own Irish bled prodigally and nobly; they have sealed their duty to their king and country by the sacrifice of nearly two thousand of their comrades. . . . In parting with the remains of that corps, in which Sir Hugh Gough has served twenty-two years, at the head of which, and by whose valour and discipline, he has obtained those marks of distinction with which he has been honoured by his royal master, he cannot too emphatically express the most heartfelt acknowledgements and his deep regret. From all classes of his officers he has uniformly experienced the most cordial and ready support.
>
> Their conduct in the field, while it called for the entire approbation of their commanding officer, acquired for them the best stay to military enterprise and military renown, *the confidence of their men*, and led to the accomplishment of their wishes, the approbation of their prince, the honour of their country, and the character of their corps. Every non-commissioned officer and man is equally entitled to the thanks of his commanding

officer. To all he feels greatly indebted, and he begs to assure all, that their prosperity as individuals, or as a corps, will ever be the first wish of his heart, and to promote which he will consider no sacrifice or exertion too great.

On February 1, the battalion was disbanded; 330 men were transferred to the 1st Battalion, which formed part of the Bengal Army, so that the Royal Irish Fusiliers, is the lineal descendant of the second battalion as well as of the first, and its regimental colours still bear the words 'Barrosa' and 'Tarifa' in remembrance of its Peninsular exploits. Sir Hugh Gough's official connexion with the 87th came to an end in 1817, but, as we shall see, it was renewed later in life, and his memory lives in the traditions and the legends of the regiment.

★★★★★★

Note:—It is recorded that a recruit, seeing the picture of Lord Gough, reproduced as the frontispiece of the second volume of the present work, asked who it was. 'That,' said a sergeant, 'is Lord Gough, and that is his fighting coat. After a battle, it was a perfect sight to see him shake the bullets out of that coat.'

★★★★★★

For more than two years. Sir Hugh remained on half-pay, but his services were too distinguished to permit of his continuing to be out of active employment, and on August 12, 1819, he was appointed to the command of the 22nd Regiment, which had just returned from Mauritius, On the same day he was gazetted full Colonel. The 22nd or Cheshire Regiment was of much more ancient date than the Prince s Own. It had been raised by the Duke of Norfolk after the Revolution of 1689, in order to defend the Protestant cause, and it had served in the battle of the Boyne, and at the siege of Limerick. In more recent days, it had been represented in the small force which accompanied Wolfe to the Heights of Abraham, in the skirmish on Bunker's Hill, and in the second capture of Cape Colony. During the Peninsular War it had been stationed in India. For two years after its return, the 22nd was in garrison at Northampton, with Sir Hugh Gough in command; but in the autumn of 1821, it was called to more active service, not by an outbreak of foreign war, but in view of the disturbed condition of Ireland.

The question of Catholic Emancipation seemed no nearer settlement in 1821 than it had been when Colonel Gough had written from the Peninsula deploring the prince regent's refusal to give way on the subject. It had been generally believed that the visit of George IV in August, 1821, would prove the occasion of granting the boon which had so long been craved, and the disappointment of this expectation was followed by an outburst of agrarian crime, an outburst which owed its origin to a combination of causes, religious, social, and economic.

★★★★★★

Note:—C.f. *Mr. Gregory's Letter-Box*, edited by Lady Gregory, which contains some interesting information regarding the state of Ireland at this period. The Irish history of the time remains to be written, and it is difficult to find any satisfactory general account of the subject.

★★★★★★

Judge O'Connor Morris, (*History of Ireland*), says:

The results of our rule in Ireland, during the fifteen years that followed the Union, had been, if we speak generally, these. A system of severe repression had been established, and, for the most part, affected Catholic Ireland; there had been a large growth of Orangeism favoured by the state, and stirring the passions of the Irish Protestants; divisions of religion and race had probably widened.

These were natural results of the rebellion of 1798, and of the identification of the Papacy with the French Empire, in the days when Napoleon menaced England. The end of the war might seem to inaugurate a happier era, but that event, in turn, was followed by economic troubles which opened fresh sores before the old ones had time to heal. During the long struggle with Napoleon, the food supply in this country had always been a matter of anxiety; fresh Irish land was thrown into cultivation, and the high prices which continued during the war sufficed to repay the labour of the peasantry. The population increased, and taxed to the utmost the resources of the good years. When peace came, and prices fell, it ceased to be profitable to cultivate large tracts of land; rents and wages shared in the universal decline of prosperity; and the results of this economic crisis were complicated by the added misfortune of local famines, caused by the failure of the harvests in certain districts. It was natural that the agrarian troubles which followed should, in part, take the form of a resistance to tithes, which pressed heavily upon the peasantry.

With the political causes which led to the formation of the Catholic Association we are not here concerned; the main result of the

121

discontent, as far as it affects our story, was the revival of the outrages of the 'Whiteboys.' During the Irish disturbances of the first years of the reign of George III a band of semi-organised rebels perpetrated a series of agrarian crimes as a protest against enclosures and against tithe, (Lecky's *History of Ireland in the Eighteenth Century*, vol. ii.). They were called 'Whiteboys' because of the white linen frocks which they wore partly as a kind of disguise and partly as a badge. Robbery and arson, outrages on cattle, and occasionally murder, were their ordinary methods, but they sometimes raised what amounted to petty insurrections, in the course of which they traversed the country in disciplined bands, attacked gaols, and threatened villages. They issued notices warning men to comply with their demands, adopting a judicial language which gave to them some wild and rude appearance of legality. These manifestoes were published in the name of a fictitious leader, Captain Right, who professed to guide their actions.

The movement which Sir Hugh Gough had to face was a recrudescence of Whiteboyism. The disturbed district, the charge of which was entrusted to him, was Buttevant, in county Cork, which remained his head quarters from October, 1821, to October, 1824. Detachments of the 22nd were stationed at Mallow, Bantyre, Charleville, Newmarket, and Ballyclough. The Whiteboys of 1821 were less numerous than those of sixty years before, and they rarely attempted open insurrection, preferring secret outrage. Their reputed leader was now Captain or General Rock, in whose name their proclamations were issued.

★★★★★★

Note:—A history of this fictitious personage was published in 1824, entitled *The Memoirs of Captain Rock*. It is, in effect, a history of agrarian troubles in Ireland, from the reign of Henry II to that of George IV, but it throws little light upon our period. 'Captain Rock' was in reality, a generic name for Whiteboy leaders.

★★★★★★

To illustrate the nature of the Whiteboy movement, it may be well to print an interesting specimen of the warnings they issued from time to time:

Mr. Haines, You are hereby required to take notice that the Catholic Potentates of Europe concurred at the consistory at Rome to elect me as a despotic to superintend Ireland, and to distribute public justice with impartiality to the divided people thereof. The laws given down to me are consistent thereof.

Therefore it is explicit to you or any person concerned that in the omission of so important a duty that I should be accountable at the temporal tribunal of the aforesaid monarchs and secondly at that awful tribunal where the best constructed fabrications of falsehood will be developed, and truth only shall prevail.

The aforesaid Consistorial Laws being formed at the constory in Rome it is not abstruce to any human being the inexpert he may be that human and divine justice requires a condign punishment to be inflicted on any person or persons who would be so unfortunate as to violate so Holy and profound a system. You remained obstinate in keeping the farm you hold from Mr. Jephson situate at old Two Pot House. But however its a matter of indifference to me now whether you surrender it or not this year because my inclination is to settle such offences against the 25th day of July next, I did not know at the same time that you had any more strangers but the Connells.

But my superintending magistrates whose duty it is to indogate what tendency the people may be devoted to thus informs me that your place is still a receptacle for strangers and that you have a herdsman and a dairy woman still in two pot House who are strangers which I require you will discharge before the 25th instant. But if you persist I will commit all your houses to my unextinguishable flames likewise I will drench my sword in the blood and slaughter of your cattle. To make a short conclusion I will inflame the frantic jaws of distraction to champ your person and property. Therefore comply and do not regret your obstinacy when too late.

Yonder Green Senate House to the throne of State, Ireland. May 19th, 1823.

General Rock, Governor and Defender of the Faith, &c., &c., &c., &c.

This notice was conveyed to the unfortunate Mr. Haynes in a manner sufficiently menacing. On the night of May 22, two of his cattle, in his farm near Two Pot House were hamstrung; and on the horns of one of them was fastened this notice. Mr. Haynes, who was a prosperous farmer, was wise enough to send this threatening letter to Sir Hugh Gough, and it is pleasant to note that the list of outrages for July and August contains no mention of Two Pot House. But if, in this particular instance, '*forewarned was forearmed*,' there was no lack of crimes of the nature indicated in 'General Rock's' letter. Statements as to a large number of these are preserved among Sir Hugh Gough's papers, but they are all of a type only too familiar in more recent days, and it would serve no useful purpose to repeat the unhappy tale.

For three years, the suppression of these outrages was Sir Hugh's task. The district committed to him covered a large portion of county Cork, north of the Black Water, and, as the state of the country became worse, other regiments, including, at different times the 57th and the 42nd Highlanders, were included in his command. The only incident which resembled an insurrection on a general scale took place in January, 1822, when a detachment of the 22nd Regiment, consisting of two officers and thirty men, defeated a gathering of rebels whose numbers were estimated at 3,000, and who were meditating an attack on Newmarket. The grateful inhabitants presented a silver cup to the officers, in recognition of their services.

Sir Hugh Gough's papers of this period, which have been preserved, relate chiefly to the year 1823 and contain no allusion to this skirmish, with which he himself had no personal connexion. The disorder reached its climax in 1823, when the burning of ricks and houses, and the hamstringing of cattle were very frequent. The number of instances of shooting at unpopular persons greatly increased, and one murder further stained the record of the year.

To deal with such a crisis special powers were required, and they were freely granted by the Government. The Insurrection Act placed the country practically under martial law; the Arms Act rendered the possession of arms a serious criminal offence and gave the authorities the right of search; and the *Habeas Corpus* Act was suspended.

******

Note:—It is interesting to note that, as recently as 1886, the appointment of Sir Hugh Gough to the disturbed districts of county Cork was quoted as a precedent in the House of Commons. The occasion was the selection of General Sir Redvers Buller to perform similar duties in the autumn of that year. Cf. the *Irish Times*, August 24, 1886.

******

A regular system of police had been established by the Peace Preservation Act in 1814, but Sir Hugh mainly depended upon military patrols. The disaffected area was divided into districts which were regularly patrolled, and the houses of all unpopular people and of those who had been warned by the Whiteboys were carefully watched. The results were not immediate, for it is always easy to take advantage of the weak points of such a system, and the terror to which the Whiteboys reduced the peasantry prevented their calling for aid or making any resistance when they were attacked, as it also rendered difficult the task of obtaining evidence against suspected persons. At first, the mills of law and order 'ground slowly' but, as time went on, they 'ground exceeding small.'

A considerable number of the criminals and at least two 'Captain Rocks' were captured and executed; the risk of detection and of punishment became greater, and, as the people gained confidence in the power of the Government, it became more easy to identify the perpetrators of outrages. By the month of October, 1824, the district was in a much more normal condition, and the 22nd Regiment was removed to the ease of garrison duty in Dublin.

The occasion of Sir Hugh's departure was marked by a public address expressive of the confidence which was reposed in him and acknowledging the good effects of his work. More than twelve months before, when a rumour of his approaching departure was circulated, the magistrates of the baronies of Duhallow, Fermoy, Orrery, Kilmore, and Clongibbon had sent him an address.

> We gratefully acknowledge that chiefly through your prudence, zeal, activity, and example, have we been enabled hitherto to avert those evils which were impending over us. In you. Sir, we have seen combined the prudent foresight of the commander, the upright spirit of the magistrate, the humane heart and courteous demeanor of the gentleman.

The mark of esteem now offered was wider and more representative. On October 16, 1824, a meeting of the noblemen, magistrates, and gentlemen resident in Sir Hugh Gough's district, was held at Mallow, under the presidency of the Viscount Doneraile, and an address to Sir Hugh Gough, the officers, non-commissioned officers, and men of the 22nd Regiment, was prepared. The language of the address is indicative of a depth of feeling natural at such a time:—

> On your first appointment to the command of this district, you were placed in a situation, arduous and critical, a situation which required the most active and increasing energy, joined to the most cool and deliberate judgement, and never was the union of these rare and essential qualifications more fully and

uniformly exemplified, than in your conduct on every occasion, while every evil passion of a misguided and infatuated Population was let loose in the Land, while the murderer and incendiary were destroying the lives and properties of innocent, unsuspecting and defenceless families, while social order and security were shaken to their very foundation, your persevering activity and judicious arrangements interposed a barrier against miscreant outrage, and certainly diminished though it was impossible totally to prevent the commission of crime.

Officers and men alike had won golden opinions in County Cork, and the good wishes of the people followed the regiment to Dublin. For two years longer it remained in Ireland, stationed at Dublin and afterwards at Galway, and during these two years Sir Hugh's connexion with it continued. His tenure of the command was further distinguished by the reintroduction of a system of regimental orders of merit.

★★★★★★

Note:—The first example of good conduct badges was set by General Studholme Hodgson, Colonel of the 5th Regiment (Northumberland Fusiliers), in the year 1767. The Order of Merit instituted in the 22nd Foot in 1785 was a similar distinction. It is possible that General Hodgson was imitating the medal given by General Forbes for his expedition to the Ohio in 1758, though that was not strictly regimental.

★★★★★★

The practice of rewarding good conduct while the regiment was not on active service had been commenced in 1785, but during the long revolutionary and Napoleonic wars, it had fallen into abeyance. To Sir Hugh belongs the credit of again adopting it. A good conduct badge, representing the oak leaves which are still associated with the Cheshire regiment, was worked by Lady Gough at Northampton in 1820, and it continued to be used in the regiment until the establishment of a general system of good conduct medals throughout the army.

Sir Hugh Gough's command of the 22nd Regiment came to an end in August, 1826. (For information regarding the 22nd, cf. the volume devoted to its history in Cannon's *Historical Records of the British Army*).

The regiment was broken up into six service and four depot companies. The service companies were sent to the West Indies, whither Sir Hugh, mainly for family reasons, did not wish to accompany them. In the *Army List* for September, 1826, his name appears as 'half-pay, unattached.' For eleven years he remained without active employment, and it seemed as if his military career were over. This enforced leisure, in the very prime of life, irked his restless spirit, and he made effort after effort to obtain some recognition of his claims. His hopes were raised when, on July 22, 1830, he was gazetted to the rank of Major-General, but he was doomed to disappointment, for nothing followed beyond a promotion in the Bath on the occasion of the coronation of William IV.

Sir Thomas Picton had urged his claim to the distinction of K.C.B. in the beginning of January, 1815, as a reward for his services at the Battle of the Pyrenees. The Order was at this time in process of reorganisation, and on its being remodelled. Sir Hugh Gough was made a Companion, with the understanding that his claim to the second class would be favourably considered on his attaining the rank of a general officer. This promise was fulfilled in 1831, but the commander-in-chief, Lord Hill (the Sir Rowland Hill of the Peninsula) remained deaf to all applications for employment. The most bitter disappointment of all occurred in August, 1834, when the Colonelcy of the 87th Regiment became vacant by the death of General Sir John Doyle. The hero of Tarifa and Barrosa naturally considered that his claims could be regarded as second to none, but Lord Hill selected for the appointment Major-General Sir Thomas Reynell.

So crushing was the blow that Sir Hugh was with difficulty restrained from retiring from the service by selling his regimental commission. Fortune had been very kind to him up to the close of the Peninsular War, and the long years of idleness which followed may have been his proper share of the evil chances of military life, but it was not easy to regard calmly this apparent close of a career which had opened so brilliantly. It has seldom happened to a man that his life work should be divided between his fourth and his seventh decade, and no one could have foreseen that the neglected general officer of 1834 would live to be the conqueror of the Punjab.

The long period of inaction came unexpectedly at length to an end in the year 1837, when Sir Hugh Gough was invited to accept the command of the Mysore Division of the Madras Army, with his head quarters at Bangalore. Lady Gough determined to accompany him to India, and, in the early autumn, they sailed in the *Minerva Castle*. An incident of the journey deserves to be recalled. On their way, the ship touched at Mauritius, where Sir Hugh's old regiment, the 87th, was stationed; and the enthusiasm of his reception impressed itself on the memories of all who witnessed the meeting. A companion (unconnected in any way with him or his family), of his journey wrote:

> He received a most wonderful ovation from the officers and men of his old regiment, the fighting 87th. During the time the ship lay at the Mauritius, they were in a state of wild excitement. The whole regiment followed him down to the boat, waded into the water, and would even have followed it swimming if they had not been sternly ordered back. The headlands were lined with them, still cheering, and the last we saw of the Mauritius was a bonfire with a number of their figures around it. (Letter from Captain Rutherford of the Bengal Artillery, written from Assam in 1838).

It was a grateful reminiscence of the past, and a prelude and inspiration to new service for Queen and country.

Sir Hugh landed at Madras in October, and at once proceeded to Bangalore, which continued to be his home for three years. A few letters of this period remain, but they are concerned with administrative details, and the writer's life differed in no respects from that of any other officer commanding a district in India. These three years of military life were a valuable experience after his civilian years, and they formed a useful preparation for a period of renewed service if the call should come. We shall find that call after call did come, and that to every call there was given a loyal and willing response.

Historical Record of the 87th (The Prince of Wales's Own Irish) Regiment of Foot, During the Napoleonic Period

Richard Cannon

THE FIRST BATTALION

The disturbed state of affairs on the continent of Europe in 1793, particularly in France, arising from the principles of the Revolution in that country, which threatened surrounding nations with universal anarchy, occasioned preparations to be made throughout the several countries, in order to oppose the dangerous doctrines which were then diffused under the specious terms of "Liberty and Equality."

On the 1st of February 1793, the National Convention of France, after the decapitation of King Louis XVI. on the 21st of the previous month, declared war against Great Britain and Holland. Augmentations were immediately made to the regular army, the militia was embodied, and the British people evinced their loyalty and patriotism by forming volunteer associations, and by making every exertion for the maintenance of monarchical principles, and for the defence of those institutions which had raised their country to a high position among the nations of Europe.

Upwards of fifty regiments of infantry were authorised to be raised, on this emergency, in the several parts of Great Britain and Ireland, by officers and gentlemen possessing local influence, sixteen of which regiments, *viz.* from the Seventy-Eighth to the Ninety-Third, continue at this period on the establishment of the army.

Of the officers thus honoured with the confidence of their sovereign and his government, Lieut.-Colonel John Doyle (afterwards

General Sir John Doyle, Bart., and G. C. B.) was selected, to whom a letter of service was addressed on the 18th of September 1793, authorising him to raise a regiment, to consist of ten companies of sixty rank and file in each company. The corps was speedily completed, and was designated the Eighty-Seventh, or the Prince of Wales's Irish Regiment.

The following is a copy of the *Letter of Service*, addressed by the Secretary-at-War to Major John Doyle, on the half-pay of the late One hundred and fifth regiment, dated:

War Office,
18th September 1793.

Sir,

I am commanded to acquaint you, that His Majesty approves of your raising a regiment of foot, without any allowance of levy money, to be completed within three months, upon the following terms, *viz.*:

The corps is to consist of one company of grenadiers, one of light infantry, and eight battalion companies. The Grenadier company is to consist of one captain, two lieutenants, three sergeants, three corporals, two drummers, two fifers, and fifty-seven private men. The Light Infantry company of one captain, two lieutenants, three sergeants, three corporals, two drummers, and fifty-seven men; and each battalion company of one captain, one lieutenant, and one ensign, three sergeants, three corporals, two drummers, and fifty-seven private men, together with the usual staff officers, and with a sergeant-major and quartermaster sergeant, exclusive of the sergeants above specified. The captain-lieutenant is (as usual) included in the number of lieutenants above mentioned.

The corps is to have one major with a company, and is to be under your command as major, with a company.

The pay of the officers is to commence from the dates of their commissions, and that of the non-commissioned officers and privates from the dates of their attestations.

His Majesty is pleased to leave to you the nomination of the officers of the regiment; but the lieut.-colonel and major are to be taken from the list of lieut.-colonels or majors on half-pay, or the major from a captain on full pay. Six of the captains are to be taken from the half-pay, and the other captain and the cap-

ORIGINAL UNIFORM OF THE EIGHTY-SEVENTH REGIMENT

tain-lieutenant from the list of captains or captain-lieutenants on full pay. All the lieutenants are to be taken from the half-pay; and the gentlemen recommended for ensigns are not to be under sixteen years of age.

No officer, however, is to be taken from the half-pay who received the difference on going upon the half-pay, nor is any officer coming from the half-pay to contribute any money towards the levy, but he may be required to raise such a quota of men as you may agree upon with him.

The person to be recommended for quartermaster must not be proposed for any other commission.

In case the corps should be reduced after it has been once established, the officers will be entitled to half-pay.

No man is to be enlisted above thirty-five years of age, nor under five feet five inches high. Well-made, growing lads, between sixteen and eighteen years of age, may be taken at five feet four inches.

The recruits are to be engaged without limitation as to the period or place of their service.

The non-commissioned officers and privates are to be inspected by a general officer, who will reject all such as are unfit for service, or not enlisted in conformity to the terms of this letter. In the execution of this service, I take leave to assure you of every assistance which my office can afford.

I have, &c., &c.,

(Signed)   George Yonge.

To Major John Doyle, on the half-pay of the late One hundred and Fifth regiment.

The following officers were appointed to commissions in the Eighty-Seventh regiment, *viz*.:—

Lieut.-Colonel Commandant — John Doyle.

Lieut.-Colonel — Edward Viscount Dungarvan
(afterwards Earl of Cork).

Major — Walter Hovenden.

Captains.

Honorable George Napier	Percy Freke.
Nathaniel Cookman.	Richard Thompson.
Honorable Robert Mead.	Howe Hadfield

Captain Lieutenant — James Magrath.

Lieutenants.	*Ensigns.*
John Thompson.	Fleming Kells.
William Aug. Blakeney.	William Murray.
John Wilson.	John Carrel.
Thomas Clarke.	—— Walker.

James Henry Fitz Simon.	Benjamin Johnson.
William Warren.	—— Salmon.
William Magrath.	
Barton Lodge.	

*   *   *   *   *   *

Adjutant — John L. Brock.   *Surgeon* — —— Hill.
Quartermaster — Wm. Thomson.   *Chaplain* — Edw. Berwick.

The effective numbers were quickly recruited, and the regiment was so far formed as to be considered fit to be employed on active continental service. It was consequently embarked in the summer of 1794, as part of a force under Major-General the Earl Moira, and was sent to join the British Army in Flanders, under the command of His Royal Highness the Duke of York. While on the march the Eighty-Seventh regiment was attacked on the 15th of July 1794, at the outpost of Alost, by a strong corps of the enemy's cavalry, which it repulsed, and for which act of bravery it received the thanks of the general officer in public orders. It is a circumstance worthy of being recorded in the regimental history, that the first individual of the regiment who was wounded, was the lieut.-colonel by whom it was raised. In the general orders of the Earl of Moira upon this occasion:

He expressed his admiration of the cool intrepidity with which the Eighty-Seventh regiment repulsed an attack from the enemy's cavalry, at the bridge of Alost, where its commander, Lieut.-Colonel Doyle, received two severe wounds, but would not quit his regiment, until the enemy had given up the attack.

The Duke of York, in his public letter, thus mentioned the affair:—

Headquarters, Cortyke,
15th July 1794.

Lord Moira speaks highly of the conduct of the officers and men of the Eighty-Seventh Regiment on this occasion, particularly of Lieut.-Colonel Doyle, commanding the corps, who was severely wounded.
(Signed)   Frederick.

In 1795 the Eighty-Seventh regiment was sent into Bergen-op-Zoom to be drilled; but soon after its arrival, the Dutch garrison revolted against the government, opened the gates, and joined the French, who entered with twenty thousand men, and made a capitulation with the Eighty-Seventh, the only British corps in the town, then commanded by Lord Dungarvan (afterwards Earl of Cork), Lieut.-

8.me Regiment

Colonel Doyle having been gent to England for the recovery of his wounds. The capitulation was however broken by the French, and the Eighty-Seventh were marched prisoners of war into France.

The regiment was again filled up, and, with the Tenth Foot, and some marines, was sent upon a secret expedition to the North Sea, under the command of Brigadier-General John Doyle, who had been promoted Colonel of the Eighty-Seventh, on the 3rd of May 1700, to co-operate with Admiral (the late Lord) Duncan; but, having been delayed in England until the end of September, the tempestuous weather, usual at that season of the year in those seas, dispersed the ships and email craft by which the troops were to be landed, and put an end to the object of the expedition. The troops returned to England in the ships of war, in which they embarked under the orders of Admiral Sir Richard Bickerton.

On the 14th of October 1796, the regiment embarked for the West Indies.

Spain having united with France in hostility to Great Britain, an expedition under Lieut.-General Sir Ralph Abercromby, K.B., proceeded against the Spanish island of Trinidad, which capitulated on the 18th of February 1797. No men were killed or wounded.

Lieutenant R—— Villeneuve, of the Eighth Foot, major of brigade to Brigadier-General Hompesch, was the only officer wounded, and he died of his wounds.

After the reduction of Trinidad, the force (of which the Eighty-Seventh formed part) destined for the expedition against Porto Rico, being assembled, the fleet sailed from Martinique on the 8th of April 1797, and on the 10th arrived at St. Kitt's, where it remained for a few days. On the 17th the fleet anchored off Congrejos Point, and a landing was effected on the island of Porto Rico on the following day. The troops advanced, when it was perceived that the only point on which the town could be attacked was on the eastern side, where it was defended by the castle and lines of St. Christopher, to approach which it was necessary to force a way over the lagoon which formed that side of the island.

This passage was strongly defended by two redoubts and gunboats, and the enemy had destroyed the bridge connecting, in the narrowest channel, the island with the main land. After every effort the British could never sufficiently silence the fire of the enemy, who was likewise entrenched in the rear of these redoubts, to hazard forcing the passage with so small a number of troops. It was next endeavoured to bombard the town from a point to the southward of it, near to a large magazine abandoned by the enemy. This was tried for several days without any great effect, on account of the distance. Lieut.-General Sir Ralph Abercromby, seeing that no act of vigour, or any combined operation between the sea and land services, could in any manner avail, determined to re-embark the troops, which was effected during the night of the 30th of April. Four Spanish fieldpieces were brought off, but not a sick or wounded soldier was left behind, and nothing of any value fell into the hands of the enemy. Sir Ralph Abercromby in his despatch alluded to the troops in the following terms:

The behaviour of the troops has been meritorious; they were patient under labour, regular and orderly in their conduct, and spirited when an opportunity to show it occurred.

The Eighty-Seventh had two rank and file killed, three wounded, and thirteen missing.

The regiment subsequently proceeded to St. Lucia, which had been captured from the French in May 1796.

During the year 1798, the regiment remained at St. Lucia.

In December 1799, the regiment proceeded from St. Lucia to Martinique.

The regiment was removed, in April 1800, from Martinique to Dominica.

In April 1801 the regiment embarked from Dominica for Barbadoes, and in August following proceeded to Curaçoa.

The preliminaries of peace, which had been agreed upon between Great Britain and France in the previous year, were ratified on the 27th of March 1802; but the peace which had been thus concluded was but of short duration. Napoleon Bonaparte, who had been elected First Consul of the French Republic, showed, on several occasions, that he continued to entertain strong feelings of hostility against Great Britain.

During the year 1802, the regiment continued to be stationed at Curaçoa.

After a few months, during which further provocations took place between the two countries, war was declared against France on the 18th of May 1803. The preparations which had been making in the French ports, the assembling of large bodies of troops on the coast, and the forming of numerous flotillas of gun-boats, justified the British government in adopting the strongest measures of defence, and in

QUEEN'S COLOUR TOP; REGIMENTAL COLOUR BOTTOM

calling upon the people for their aid and services. Numerous volunteer associations were formed in all parts of the kingdom in defence of the Sovereign, the laws, and the institutions of the country. The militia was re-embodied, and the regular army was considerably augmented, under the *Army of Reserve Act.*

The Eighty-Seventh regiment embarked from the island of Curaçoa for England on the 12th of January 1803, on board of the ship *De Ruyter*, which, meeting with tempestuous weather, was obliged to put into Jamaica, from whence it proceeded to Antigua, where it arrived in April 1803. The regiment proceeded to St. Kitt's in June following.

On the 28th of July 1804 the regiment embarked from St. Kitt's, and on the 28th of September following it landed at Plymouth, after a service of eight years in the West Indies, having lost during that period, by the diseases incident to the climate, many officers, and between seven and eight hundred men.

On the 31st of October the regiment embarked, under the command of Lieut.-Colonel Sir Edward Butler, from Plymouth, for Guernsey, of which island Major-General Doyle had been appointed to the command and to the Lieutenant-Governorship.

The British Government, having ascertained that the King of Spain had engaged to furnish powerful aid to France, felt itself compelled to consider Spain as an enemy, and accordingly issued orders for intercepting some frigates off Cadiz, which were on their way to France with cargoes of treasure: a declaration of war was consequently issued by the Court of Madrid against Great Britain on the 12th of December 1804.

The establishment of the Eighty-Seventh regiment, which had been authorised to receive men raised in certain counties of Ireland, under the Act of Parliament, dated 14th July 1804, termed the *Additional Force Act* was augmented by a second battalion.

THE SECOND BATTALION

The British Government continued to adopt the most vigorous measures for the defence of the kingdom, and for the prosecution of the war. In addition to the acts of Parliament passed in July 1803 for raising *The Army of Reserve* further Acts were passed in June and July 1804 for levying a larger number of men in the several counties of Great Britain and Ireland, which were termed the *Additional Force Acts.*

The Eighty-Seventh regiment, was augmented by a second battalion, which, with seven other regiments, was appointed to receive men raised in Ireland under the act of the 14th of July 1804; the men raised in the counties of Tipperary, Galway, and Clare, were allotted to the Eighty-Seventh regiment; the assembling quarter of the second battalion was appointed at Frome in Somersetshire, and the battalion was placed on the establishment of the army, from the 25th of December 1804, at six hundred rank and file, which was augmented in the following year to eight hundred, and in the year 1807 to one thousand rank and file, and continued at that number to December 1814, when it was reduced to eight hundred, and from December 1815 to six hundred rank and file.

The second battalion marched from Frome to Bristol in March 1805, and embarked for Ireland.

On the 27th of October 1806 the battalion, consisting of twenty-nine sergeants, nine drummers, and five hundred and sixty-eight rank and file, embarked from Ireland for England.

On the 27th of April 1807 the battalion embarked at Plymouth, and proceeded to Guernsey.

The following report was made to Lieut.-General Sir John Doyle, Bart., commanding the troops at Guernsey, by Brigadier-General John Fraser, after his inspection of the second battalion of the Eighty-Seventh regiment.

Guernsey, 30th June 1807.

Sir,

I have the honour to report, that when I minutely inspected the second battalion of the Eighty-Seventh regiment two months after their arrival in this island, I found every thing in a state of perfection that would have done credit to an old established regiment, and which could not have been expected in a battalion so lately formed. The flank companies are uncommonly fine. The battalion men are in general of good size, young and stout, and the whole appear healthy and well fed: they march well, are steady under arms, and perfect in their discipline. The interior regulations are excellent, barracks and hospital clean, books regular, women and children decent in their appearance, *and everything to be commended.* The appointments are in good order, the clothing is very good and well fitted, gaiters, shoes, &c. good without exception. There have been very few courts martial, very few non-commissioned officers reduced, and *not one punished man in the battalion.*

The officers are well dressed and very attentive to their duty. Since their arrival here, the Eighty-Seventh have occupied the town district, where I have had daily opportunities of seeing them, and I have always found them attentive on duty, well dressed in the streets, quiet and regular, no complaints, no drunkenness, even at the monthly settlements.

I am of opinion that the second battalion of the Eighty-Seventh is fit for any service, and very likely to be distinguished, especially while commanded by Lieut.-Colonel Doyle, who appears one of the best and most attentive officers I have ever seen, and who is to be particularly commended for keeping up very strict discipline without the least appearance of severity.

I have, &c.,

(Signed)   John Fraser,
                                                         Brigadier-General.

To Lieut-General Sir John Doyle, Bart., commanding His Majesty's Forces in Guernsey and Alderney.

The above report of Brigadier-General Fraser was highly gratifying to His Royal Highness the Duke of York, Commander-in-Chief, whose approbation thereof was signified to Lieut.-Colonel Doyle, and to the second battalion, through Lieut.-General Sir John Doyle, by the adjutant-general on the 10th of July 1807.

Important events had in the meantime occurred on the continent of Europe. Napoleon having reduced Germany to submission to his will, and forced Russia to accede to his decrees, next attempted the subjugation of Spain and Portugal. The Spaniards and Portuguese rose in arms to assert their national rights, the French emperor having conferred the crown of Spain on his brother Joseph, who relinquished the throne of Naples in favour of Marshal Murat. In the summer of Portugal was delivered by a British Army under Lieut.-General Sir Arthur Wellesley, and in the autumn Lieut.-General Sir John Moore received orders to advance with a body of British troops from Portugal into the heart of Spain; several regiments were embarked from the United Kingdom to co-operate in the enterprise.

On the 4th of June 1808, the battalion embarked from Guernsey, proceeded to Harwich, and from thence to Ramsgate, having previously occupied Weely Barracks and Danbury Camp.

Lieut.-Colonel Charles W. Doyle having been appointed a brigadier general and employed on a special mission in Spain, the command of the second battalion devolved upon Major Hugh Gough, and on the 28th of December following, it embarked at Ramsgate to join the army under Lieut.-General Sir John Moore, with numerous supplies of men and stores; but being dispersed by a storm, it rendezvoused at Cork, from whence it was ordered to proceed to Portugal.

The battalion arrived at Lisbon on the 12th of March 1809, and joined the army under the command of Lieut.-General Sir Arthur Wellesley. It was employed in the operations against the French at Oporto, and advanced in April following in pursuit of the French army, which had retreated from Portugal towards Madrid.

After suffering many privations in common with the rest of the troops, a junction was effected at Oropesa on the 20th of July with the Spanish Army under General Cuesta. On the 27th of July, when General Cuesta had retreated from Alcabon under cover of Lieut.-General Sherbrooke's divisions, Lieut.-General Sir Arthur Wellesley, K.B., withdrew to the position of Talavera, leaving Major-General John Randoll McKenzie on the Alberche to protect the movement. When the French on the 27th of July crossed this river, Major-General McKenzie's division was posted near the Casa des Salinas, his infantry in the forest, and cavalry on the plain.

The attack was somewhat sudden, and the second battalions of the Thirty-First and Eighty-Seventh regiments, which were in the wood on the right of the Alberche, sustained some loss. As the enemy increased his numbers on the British side of the river, Major-General McKenzie fell back gradually, and entering the position by the left of the combined army, took up his ground in a second line in rear of the foot guards. In the dusk of the evening the enemy commenced his attack on the British left, but failed. In the night the attack was repeated, and on the morning of the 28th of July the French renewed the attack on the height on the British left, and were again repulsed with considerable loss.

After a pause of some hours the attacks were renewed upon the whole British front, and the action became general. Brigadier-General Alexander Campbell's division, on the British right, sustained the assault of the enemy's fourth corps, assisted by Major-General McKenzie's brigade.

The English regiments, putting the French skirmishers aside, met the advancing columns with loud shouts, and breaking in on their front, and lapping their flanks with fire, and giving no

144

respite, pushed them back with a terrible carnage. Ten guns were taken; but as General Campbell prudently forbore pursuit, the French rallied on their supports, and made a show of attacking again. Vain attempt! The British artillery and musketry played too vehemently upon their masses, and a Spanish regiment of cavalry charging on their flank at the same time, the whole retired in disorder, and the victory was secured in that quarter. (Lieut.-General Sir William Napier's *History of the Peninsular War*).

In the action on the 28th of July, Major-General McKenzie, who commanded the division of which the Eighty-Seventh formed part, was killed.

The news of the victory of Talavera gained over the French army, commanded by Joseph Bonaparte in person, excited great joy in England, and Lieut.-General Sir Arthur Wellesley was raised to the peerage by the title of Viscount Wellington.

The loss of the British amounted to six thousand in killed, wounded, and missing; that of the French was much more considerable. The loss sustained by the second battalion of the Eighty-Seventh regiment consisted of one officer and one hundred and ten men killed, and thirteen officers and two hundred and thirty men wounded: total three hundred and fifty-four; strength in the field, eight hundred and twenty-six, leaving a remainder of four hundred and seventy-two.

Killed.

Ensign — Nicholas la Serre.

Wounded.

Major — Hugh Gough, *severely* (on 28th July).
Captain — Rawdon Mᶜ Crea, *slightly* (*since dead*).
    „   Anthony William Somersall, *slightly*.
Lieutenant — W. G. Cavanagh, *severely*.
    „   Richard Thos. Hingston, *died of his wounds*.
    „   Ralph Johnson, *severely*.
    „   John D. Bagenal, *arm amputated*.
    „   James Carroll, *severely*.
    „   Adam Rogers, *severely* (on 28th July).
Ensign — Theobald Butler, *severely*.
    „   Theobald Pepper, *severely* (on 28th July).
    „   Wright Knox, *severely*.
    „   James T. Moore, *slightly*.

Acting Sergeant-Major Paterson was promoted to an ensigncy for good conduct in .this action, and Quartermaster Sergeant Cowell was shortly afterwards promoted also to an ensigncy for length of service and gallant conduct.

The Eighty-Seventh subsequently received the royal authority to bear the word "Talavera," on the regimental colour and appointments, in commemoration of the conduct of the second battalion on that occasion.

The junction of the divisions of Marshals Soult, Ney, and Mortier, in the rear of the British, compelled them to fall back on Badajoz. On the 10th of September, the second battalion of the Eighty-Seventh regiment received orders to repair to Lisbon, where it arrived on the 24th; and two strong detachments having arrived from England, and a number of wounded men joining from the hospitals, the battalion was again reported fit for service.

On the 5th of February 1810, the battalion embarked at Lisbon for Cadiz, and disembarked there on the 12th, which city was at that time besieged by a powerful French Army, under Marshal Soult. The whole of this year the battalion was employed in erecting batteries, and strengthening the defence of the place, during which the battalion lost several men.

Lieut.-General Thomas Graham (afterwards Lord Lynedoch) commanded the British forces in Cadiz, and an expedition was resolved upon for the purpose of making a combined attack on the rear of the blockading army under Marshal Victor, who now commanded at the siege of Cadiz, in consequence of Marshal Soult having proceeded with a body of troops into Estremadura.

On the 18th of February 1811, the battalion embarked at Cadiz, and sailed for Gibraltar.

The army under the command of Lieut.-General Graham consisted of about three thousand men, (see list following), and a body of seven thousand troops commanded by General La Pena.

The following corps were employed in the Battle of Barrosa on the 5th of March 1811, *viz.*

2nd Hussars, King's German Legion.	47th Foot, 2nd batt. (flank comp.)
Royal Artillery.	67th Foot, 2nd batt.
Royal Engineers.	82nd Foot, 2nd batt. (flank comp)
1st Foot Guards, 2nd batt.	87th Foot, 2nd batt.
Coldstream Guards, 2nd batt.	Rifle Brigade { 2nd batt.
3rd Foot Guards, 2nd batt.	{ 3rd batt.
9th Foot, 1st batt. (flank companies.)	20th Portuguese Regiment.
28th Foot, 1st batt.	Royal Staff Corps, 1 comp.

The force of which the Eighty-Seventh formed part, disembarked at Algesiras on the 23rd of February, and the troops being united at Tarifa, marched from thence on the 28th of February.

General Zayas pushed a strong body of Spanish troops across the river Santi Petri near the coast on the 1st of March, threw a bridge over, and formed a *tête-de-pont*. This post was attacked by the enemy on the nights of the 3rd and 4th of March, who was repulsed, though the Spaniards sustained considerable loss.

On the 5th of March 1811, Lieut.-General Graham, and the army under his command, arrived on the low ridge of Barrosa, and gained a decisive victory over the French army under Marshal Victor, composed of the two divisions of Generals Rufin and Laval.

The circumstances under which Lieut.-General Graham found himself placed were such as compelled him to attack the very superior force, in point of numbers, of his opponents. The allied army, after a night-march of sixteen hours from the camp near Veger, arrived on the morning of the 5th at the low ridge of Barrosa, about four miles to the southward of the mouth of the Santi Petri river. This height extends inland about a mile and a half, continuing on the north the extensive heathy plain of Chiclana. A great pine forest skirts the plain, and circles round the height at some distance, terminating down to Santi Petri, the intermediate space between the north side of the height and the forest being uneven and broken.

A well-conducted and successful attack on the rear of the enemy's lines near Santi Petri by the vanguard of the Spaniards under Brigadier-General Ladrizabel, opened the communication with the Isla de Leon, and Lieut.-General Graham received General La Pena's directions to move down from the position of Barrosa to that of the Torre de Bermeja, about half way to the Santi Petri river, in order to secure the communication across the river, over which a bridge had been recently constructed. This latter position occupied a narrow woody ridge, the right on the sea cliff, the left falling down to the Almanza creek on the edge of the marsh. An easy communication between the western points of these two positions was kept up by a hard sandy beach. Lieut.-General Graham, while on the march through the wood towards the Bermeja, received intelligence that the enemy had appeared in force on the plain of Chiclana, about fifty miles from Tarifa, and was advancing towards the heights of Barrosa.

The British general, considering that position as the key to that of Santi Petri, immediately countermarched in order to support the troops left for its defence, and the alacrity with which this manoeuvre was executed served as a favourable omen. It was, however, impossible in such intricate and difficult ground to preserve order in the columns, and time was never afforded to restore it entirely.

Before the British could get quite disentangled from the wood, the troops on the Barrosa hill were seen returning from it, while the enemy's left wing was rapidly ascending. His right wing at the same time stood on the plain, on the edge of the wood, within cannon-shot. A retreat in the face of such an enemy, already within reach of the easy communication by the sea-beach, must have involved the whole allied army in all the danger of being attacked during the unavoidable confusion of the different corps arriving nearly at the same time on the narrow ridge of the Bermeja.

Lieut.-General Graham relying on the heroism of British troops, and regardless of the number arid position of the enemy, determined on an immediate attack. Major Duncan soon opened a powerful battery of ten guns in the centre. The right wing proceeded to the attack of General Rufin's division on the hill, while that under General Laval, notwithstanding the havoc made by Major Duncan's battery, continued to advance in very imposing masses, opening his fire of musketry, and was only checked by that of the left wing.

The left wing now advanced firing; and a most determined charge by the three companies of Guards and the second battalion of the Eighty-Seventh regiment, supported by the remainder of the wing, soon decided the defeat of General Laval's division. In this charge the Eagle of the eighth French regiment of light infantry (which suffered immensely) and a howitzer were captured, and remained in possession of Major Gough, now Lieut.-General Viscount Gough, G.C.B., and colonel of the Eighty-Seventh regiment.

★★★★★★

Note:—In the midst of the engagement, Sergeant Patrick Masterson seized and kept possession of the Eagle of the eighth French regiment of light infantry (which was the first taken in action since the commencement of the Peninsular War), and for which His Royal Highness the Prince Regent promoted the sergeant to an ensigncy in the Royal York Light Infantry Volunteers; he was subsequently removed to the Eighty-Seventh regiment.

Volunteer de Courcy Ireland, and Sergeant-Major McKeldon, were also promoted to be ensigns for their conduct in this action.

★★★★★★

The French Imperial Eagle
Of the 8th Regiment,
Taken by His MAJESTY'S 2nd Battalion 87th (or Prince of Wales Irish)
under the command of Major Hugh Gough

These attacks were zealously supported by Colonel Belson with the Twenty-Eighth, and Lieut.-Colonel Prevost with a portion of the Sixty-Seventh regiment.

A reserve formed beyond the narrow valley, across which the enemy was closely pursued, next shared the same fate, and was routed by the same means.

The right wing meanwhile was not less successful, and, after a sanguinary contest, General Rufin's division was driven from the heights in confusion, leaving two pieces of cannon. In less than an hour and a half from the commencement of the action, the French were in full retreat. The retiring division met, halted, and seemed inclined to form; but a new and more advanced position of the British artillery quickly dispersed the enemy. The exhausted state of the troops rendered pursuit impossible, and a position was occupied on the eastern side of the hill. When the conflict had ceased, Lieut.-General Graham remained on the field of battle but the Spanish general, La Pena, who had looked on while this terrible battle was fought, did not seize the favourable opportunity which the valour of the British troops had put into his hands, of striking a severe blow at the remains of the French army retreating in disorder. The inactivity of the Spaniards continuing, the British proceeded to Cadiz on the following day.

In this battle the Eighty-Seventh had one officer and forty-four men killed; four officers and one hundred and twenty-four men wounded: the strength of the battalion in the field was seven hundred and twenty-two.

Killed.

Ensign — Edward E. Kough.

Wounded.

Major — Archibald Maclaine.

Captain — Anthony William Somersall.

Lieutenant — James Gubbins Fennell.

    ,,   James Campbell Barton.

Lieut.-General Graham stated, in his public despatch:

No expressions of mine could do justice to the conduct of the troops throughout. Nothing less than the almost unparalleled exertions of every officer, the invincible bravery of every soldier, and the most determined devotion to the honour of His Majesty's arms, in all, could have achieved this brilliant success, against such a formidable enemy so posted.

Among the prisoners were the General of Division Rufin, the General of Brigade Rousseau; the Chief of the Staff, General Bellegarde; an *aide-de-camp* of Marshal Victor; the Colonel of the Eighth regiment, and several other officers. The prisoners amounted to two general officers, one field officer, nine captains, eight subalterns, and four hundred and twenty rank and file. The enemy lost about three thousand men in killed, wounded, and prisoners, while that of the British amounted to one thousand two hundred and forty-three killed and wounded. Six pieces of cannon were also captured.

Lieut.-General Graham, on this glorious occasion, wrote a short but comprehensive note from the field of battle, to General Sir John Doyle, the colonel of the Eighty-Seventh regiment, in these words, congratulating him on the steadiness and gallantry displayed by the second battalion in an action which redounded so much to the fame of the British arms.

Barrosa, 5th March, 1811.

My Dear Doyle,
Your regiment has covered itself with glory. Recommend it and its commander (Gough) to their illustrious patron, the Prince Regent: too much cannot be done for it.
Ever yours,
(Signed)   T. Graham.

Major Hugh Gough was promoted to the brevet rank of Lieut.-Colonel, in consequence of Lieut.-General Graham's recommendation, for his gallantry at Barrosa, and also received a medal for that battle.

On the 18th of April 1811, His Royal Highness the Prince Regent was pleased to approve of the Eighty-Seventh being in future styled "The Eighty-Seventh, or Prince of Wales's Own Irish Regiment" and of its bearing, as a badge of honour, on the regimental colour and appointments an eagle with a wreath of laurel above the harp, in addition to the arms of His Royal Highness, in commemoration of the distinguished gallantry of the second battalion on various occasions, and particularly at the Battle of Barrosa on the 5th of March 1811.

Both Houses of Parliament unanimously voted their thanks to Lieut.-General Graham, and the officers and men under his command, for this victory, and their valour and ability were highly applauded by the nation.

The importance of the victory was fully appreciated by Lieut.-General Viscount Wellington, K. B., who in a letter to Lieut.-General Graham, of the 25th of March, thus expressed himself:—

I beg to congratulate you and the brave troops under your command, on the signal victory which you gained on the 5th instant. I have no doubt whatever, that their success would have had the effect of raising the siege of Cadiz, if the Spanish corps had made any effort to assist them; and I am equally certain, from your account of the ground, that if you had not decided with the utmost promptitude to attack the enemy, and if your attack had not been a most vigorous one, the whole allied army would have been lost.

You have to regret that such a victory should not have been followed by all the consequences which might reasonably be expected from it; but you may console yourself with the reflection that you did your utmost, and, at all events, saved the allied army; and that the failure in the extent of benefit to be derived from your exertions is to be attributed to those who would have derived most advantage from them.

I concur in the propriety of your withdrawing to the Isla on the 6th, as much as I admire the promptitude and determination of your attack of the 5th; and I most sincerely congratulate you and the brave troops under your command, on your success.

And in a letter of the same date to Marshal Sir William Carr Beresford, K.B., Viscount Wellington stated:—

General Graham has returned to the Isla, after having fought the hardest action that has been fought yet. The Spaniards left him very much to his own exertions. The Spanish general is to be brought to a court-martial.

In a letter of the 27th of March to the Earl of Liverpool, Secretary of State, Lieut.-General Viscount Wellington expressed similar sentiments to the foregoing, and added:—

I am convinced that His Royal Highness the Prince Regent will duly appreciate the promptitude with which Lieut.-General Graham decided to attack the enemy in the important position of which they had obtained possession; the vigour with which he carried that decision into execution, and the gallantry displayed by all the officers and troops upon that glorious occasion.

The Eighty-Seventh having returned to Cadiz, after the Battle of Barrosa, remained there until the 10th of October, when it embarked with a brigade under the command of Colonel Skerrett, of the Forty-Seventh regiment, and landed at Tarifa on the 15th of that month. A strong division of the French Army, amounting to ten thousand men, under the immediate orders of General Laval, invested the town of Tarifa on the 20th of December 1811. The garrison consisted of a thousand British, and about seven hundred Spanish troops, and was commanded by Colonel Skerrett. In the night of the 29th the enemy fired salvos of grape on the breach, and on the 30th the breaching fire was renewed. A heavy rain filled the bed of the river during the night, and the torrent bringing down planks, fascines, gabions and dead bodies from the French camp, broke the palisades, and bent the portcullis backward. The surge of the waters also injured the defences behind the breach. After a heavy cannonading and bombardment, with considerable skirmishing, a breach in the walls was effected, and preparations were made for storming on the 31st of December.

The post of the Eighty-Seventh was at the breach; and about eight o'clock in the morning of the 31st, the French troops, amounting to two thousand chosen men, composed of all the grenadiers and *voltigeurs* of the army, advanced thereto, where they were received by the Eighty-Seventh with three cheers, the battalion at the same time pouring in a most tremendous and well directed fire, which, for a moment, checked the enemy, who, as if to escape the fire, ran with desperation towards the breach, which they found impracticable; they then hurried along the wall, to endeavour to force the portcullis, but without effect, on which they fled precipitately to their own lines.

During the attack, the drums and fifes of the regiment played the favourite Irish airs of *Patrick's Day* and *Garryowen*, and nothing but the steadiness and discipline of the corps could have prevented them from pursuing the enemy.

The following eloquent description of this assault is given by Lieut.-General Sir William Napier, K. C. B., in his *History of the Peninsular War.*

The waters subsided in the night as quickly as they had risen, but at daylight a living stream of French grenadiers glided swiftly down the bed of the river, and as if assured of victory,

A SERGEANT and PRIVATES of the 87th

OR PRINCE of WALES'S OWN IRISH REGIMENT on SERVICE.

arrived, without shout or tumult, within a few yards of the walls, when, instead of quitting the hollow, to reach the breach, they, like the torrent of the night, continued their rapid course, and dashed against the portcullis. The British soldiers who had hitherto been silent and observant, as if at a spectacle which they were expected to applaud, now arose, and with a crashing volley smote the head of the French column.

The leading officer, covered with wounds, fell against the portcullis, and gave up his sword through the bars to Colonel Gough. The French drummer, a gallant boy, who was beating the charge, dropped lifeless by his officer's side, and the dead and wounded filled the hollow. The remainder of the assailants then breaking out to the right and left, spread along the slopes of ground under the ramparts, and opened a quick irregular musketry.

At the same time, a number of men coming out of the trenches, leaped into pits digged in front, and shot fast at the garrison, but no escalade or diversion at the other points was made, and the storming column was dreadfully shattered; for the ramparts streamed forth fire, and from the north-eastern tower a field-piece, held in reserve expressly for the occasion, sent, at pistol-shot distance, a tempest of grape whistling through the French masses, which were swept away in such a dreadful manner, that they could no longer endure the destruction, but plunging once more into the hollow returned to their camp, while a shout of victory, mingled with the sound of musical instruments, passed round the wall of the town.

This gallant affair cost the regiment but little; Lieutenants M. Carroll and Waller being the only officers wounded, and a few of the men.

Volunteer William Ireland was promoted to an ensigncy for his own good conduct and that of the regiment at the siege of Tarifa; and Sergeant Irwin very much distinguished himself.

The following is the return of killed and wounded in the action at Tarifa on the 31st of December:—

Royal Engineers.—Lieutenant Joseph Longley, killed.

Forty-Seventh Regiment, Second Battalion.—Lieutenant Richard Hall and one man killed; Lieutenant George Hill and two rank and file wounded.

Eighty-Seventh Regiment, Second Battalion.—Five rank and

file killed; Lieutenant Morgan Carroll, Ensign Waller, and twenty-one rank and file wounded.

Ninety-Fifth Regiment, Second Battalion (Rifles.)—One man killed, and one wounded.

Total.—Two officers, and seven rank and file killed: three officers, and twenty-four rank and file wounded.

Colonel Skerrett, in the evening, issued the following orders:—

Colonel Skerrett most sincerely congratulates the British garrison on the glorious result of the affair of today. Two thousand of the enemy's best troops attacked the breach, and were totally defeated with immense loss. On our side all behaved nobly; but the onduct of Lieut.-Colonel Gough, and the Eighty-Seventh regiment, surpasses praise.

The situation of the enemy's wounded, with which the ground was covered between his battery and the British fire, where they must have inevitably perished, induced Colonel Skerrett, from motives of compassion, to hoist a flag of truce to carry them off. Some were brought into the place over the breach; but from the extreme difficulty attending this, the French were allowed to carry the remainder away. General Laval expressed his acknowledgment of the conduct of the British and Spanish nations on this occasion in the most feeling and grateful terms. The enemy's loss was very severe, and ten officers were amongst the prisoners.

★★★★★★

Note:—In a letter, dated the 21st of January 1812, from General Viscount Wellington, K.B., to the Earl of Liverpool, Secretary of State, appeared the following tribute from that illustrious commander to the conduct of the troops at Tarifa:—"I cannot refrain from expressing my admiration of the conduct of Colonel Skerrett, and the brave troops under his command, nor from recommending them to the protection of your Lordship."

★★★★★★

From the movements of the enemy on the 4th of January 1812, it was supposed that another assault was intended, and the garrison waited in eager expectation to display another proof of British valour. On the following morning, at daylight, the columns of the enemy were already at a distance, having taken advantage of a dark and stormy night to make a precipitate retreat, leaving in the possession of the British all his artillery, ammunition, and stores. Marshal Victor was present in the French camp to give orders for the retreat. Major Richard Broad, with a part of the Forty-Seventh regiment, was immediately ordered to follow the enemy, and he took possession of the artillery, waggons, and a quantity of stores in sufficient time to save them from the flames, the French having set fire to them. Some prisoners were made on this occasion. In an intercepted despatch from Marshal Soult, three months after the siege, it was stated:—

> The taking of Tarifa will be more hurtful to the English and to the defenders of Cadiz, than the taking of Alicant or even Badajoz, where I cannot go without first securing my left and taking Tarifa. (*History of the War in the Peninsular and in the South of France*, by Lieut.-General Sir William Napier, K.C. B.).

The royal authority was afterwards granted for the Eighty-Seventh to bear the word "Tarifa" on the regimental colour and appointments, in commemoration of the distinguished gallantry of the second battalion in successfully defending the breach at that place against a very superior French force on the 31st of December 1811.

Four companies being left in Tarifa, the six companies returned to Cadiz, the siege of which place having been raised, the six companies marched in August 1812 with other corps from Cadiz, and occupied Seville, where they were shortly joined by the four companies from Tarifa. The battalion quitted Seville on the 30th of September, in order to join the army under the Marquis of Wellington, to which it was transferred on the first of October 1812.

The battalion proceeded to join the fourth division of the Peninsular army at Aranjuez, near Madrid, on the 25th of October. On the morning of the 31st, at eight o'clock, the advanced guard of Marshal Soult, consisting of nine thousand men, attacked the passage of the bridge and fort of Puerto Largo, several times during the day, but was defeated with considerable loss.

The second battalion of the Eighty-Seventh regiment on this occasion behaved with great gallantry, and, continuing its march to Madrid, reached it that night, but, on the following one, commenced its retreat to Salamanca, during which the rear-guard, being formed by the third brigade, of which the Eighty-Seventh then composed a part, was, on the 16th of November, attacked several times by the enemy's cavalry. In the end of December, the regiment arrived at Salamanca, having lost during the retreat to Portugal, two officers, namely,

Ensigns De Courcy Ireland and William Ireland, eight sergeants, two drummers, and one hundred and eighty-two rank and file, by disease caused by fatigue and extreme bad weather. It rained continually for three days and nights, during which the regiment had no tents to cover them. The men were obliged to sit down in line each night to receive the enemy.

Sergeants Coppin, M'Mahon, Milligan, O'Hara, and Palmer, were promoted to be ensigns after the retreat, on account of the good conduct of the regiment.

A striking instance of intrepidity and presence of mind occurred on one of those marches in the Peninsula, which so frequently terminated in a general action. During a short halt, the Eighty-Seventh took up its ground upon a hill not far from the enemy, and the men were sitting down to rest, when a howitzer, that had been masked, opened upon them; some shells fell short, but one alighted in the centre of one of the companies. The men naturally endeavoured to get out of its reach, when James Geraghty, a private grenadier, called out to the men, "that he would show them how they played football at Limerick;" and immediately kicked the live shell, with its burning fuse, over the edge of the hill: the moment it touched the ground it exploded without, injuring a man of the regiment. For this gallant act the commanding officer made the man a handsome present.

The army took the field in 1813, and arrived in the neighbourhood of Vittoria on the 18th of June, and on the 21st of that month the regiment was engaged with the French Army until dark, when the enemy was routed with immense loss; one hundred and fifty-one pieces of artillery, a stand of colours, with all his baggage, falling into the hands of the victors.

The Eighty-Seventh formed part of the third division; the Marquis of Wellington ordered that an attack should be made on three separate points; on the right by Lieut.-General Sir Rowland Hill, with the second division, upon the French left at Puebla; while on the left, Lieut.-General Sir Thomas Graham, with the first and fifth divisions, was to make a wide detour to the left, and crossing the Zadorra at Vittoria to attack their right, and cut off their retreat by the great road to Bayonne. The centre, consisting of the fourth and light divisions (under the Marquis of Wellington himself) on the right, and the third and seventh (under Lieut.-General the Earl of Dalhousie) on the left, were to pass the bridges in front, and attack as soon as the movements on the flanks should be executed. The difficult nature of the country

160

prevented the communication between the different columns moving to the attack from their stations on the River Bayas, at as early an hour as was expected.

The fourth and light divisions, however, passed the Zadorra immediately after Lieut.-General Sir Rowland Hill had obtained possession of Subijana de Alava; and almost as soon as these had crossed, the column under the Earl of Dalhousie arrived at Mendoza. The third division, under Lieut.-General Sir Thomas Picton, crossed at the bridge higher up, followed by the seventh division under the Earl of Dalhousie. The seventh division, and the centre brigade of the third division, then attacked the French right centre, in front of the villages of Margarita and Hermandad; and the Marquis of Wellington, seeing the hill in front of the village of Arinez weakly occupied by the enemy, ordered the right brigade of the third division, under Lieut.-General Sir Thomas Picton, in close columns of battalions, at a run diagonally across the front of both armies, to that central point.

The hill was carried immediately, and the French withdrew, under cover of a cannonade from fifty pieces of artillery and a crowd of skirmishers, to the second range of heights on which their reserve had been posted; they, however, still held the village of Arinez, on the great road leading to Vittoria. The brigade then advanced to the attack of the village of Arinez, and the French were finally driven back in confusion at the point of the bayonet. These four divisions, forming the centre of the army, were destined to attack the height on which the right of the enemy's centre was placed, while Lieut.-General Sir Rowland Hill should move forward from Subijana de Alava to attack the left. The enemy, however, having weakened his line to strengthen his detachment on the hills, abandoned his position in the valley as soon as he saw the British position to attack it, and ultimately commenced his retreat in good order towards Vittoria.

Notwithstanding the difficulty of the ground, the allied troops continued to advance in admirable order, Other movements took place, the result of which terminated in a complete victory. King Joseph, whose carriage and court equipage were seized, had barely time to escape on horseback. The defeat was the most complete that the French had sustained in the Peninsula.

The Marquis of Wellington, in his despatch, stated that:—

Major-General the Honourable Charles Colville's brigade of the third division was seriously attacked in its advance by a very superior force well formed, which it drove in, supported by General Inglis's brigade of the seventh division, commanded by Colonel Grant, of the Eighty-Second. *These officers and the troops under their command distinguished themselves.*

In this conflict the Eighty-Seventh, under Lieut. Colonel Gough, had the honour of taking the *bâton* of Marshal Jourdan. The circumstance was thus alluded to upon the Marquis of Wellington being appointed a Field Marshal. In a most flattering letter, the Prince Regent, in the name and behalf of His Majesty, thus conferred the honour:—

> Your have sent me among the trophies of your unrivalled fame the staff of a French Marshal, and I send you in return that of England.

The Eighty-Seventh had one ensign, four sergeants, and eighty-three rank and file killed; three captains, four lieutenants, two ensigns, seven sergeants, two drummers, and one hundred and forty-eight rank and file wounded, making a total of two hundred and fifty-four. The strength of the battalion in the field was six hundred and thirty-seven.

Killed.

Ensign — Walter O'Grady.

Wounded.

Captain —Frederick Vandeleur, ⎫
    „   James O'Brien, ⎬ *died of their wounds.*
    „   James King.

Lieutenant — Philip Higginson.
    „   William Mountgarrett.
    „   Thomas Dowling.
    „   Wright Knox.

Ensign — John Stafford.
    „   Hilliard.

The royal authority was subsequently granted for the word "Vittoria" to be borne on the regimental colour and appointments of the Eighty-Seventh, in commemoration of the gallantry of the second battalion in this battle.

Volunteer O'Grady, and Sergeant Major Wallace, were promoted for their good conduct; and Lieutenant and Adjutant Moore had two horses shot under him in this battle.

The army pursued the French, who, after throwing in reinforcements into the fortress of Pampeluna, continued their retreat. Being reinforced, and Marshal Soult, who had been selected by Napoleon for the command of the French Army in Spain, with the rank of "Lieutenant of the Emperor," having arrived, they forced the British to retire on a position in the Spanish range of the Pyrenees; when the brigade, in which the Eighty-Seventh was placed, held the right of the position from the 27th of July to the 1st of August, during which the enemy twice made demonstrations of attack. The French being defeated on the 1st of August, retreated and took up and fortified a position in their own territories; the British pursued through the famous pass of Roncesvalles, and on the 8th of August 1813, first came in view of France, and entered its territories on the 10th of November, having during the intermediate period being engaged in skirmishes, in which a few were killed and wounded.

On the 10th of November the British troops were engaged at the Nivelle, from five o'clock in the morning until dark, meeting with a most obstinate resistance in an entrenched camp. The gallantry of the allies, however, drove the French to Saint Jean de Luz. The Eighty-Seventh on this occasion called forth from Major-General the Honourable Charles Colville, who commanded the division, and Colonel John Keane (afterwards Lieut.-General Lord Keane), who commanded the brigade, the most animated praises. One ensign, six sergeants, one drummer, and sixty-eight rank and file, were killed; one lieut.-colonel, four lieutenants, eleven sergeants, one drummer, and one hundred and twenty-three rank and file, wounded. Total, two hundred and sixteen. The strength of the battalion in the field was three hundred and eighty-six.

Killed.
Ensign — Hilliard.

Wounded.
Brevet Lieut.-Colonel — Hugh Gough.
Lieutenant — John Kelly, *leg amputated.*
    „   Joseph Leslie.
    „   James Kenelly.
Ensign — Henry Bailey.

The word "Nivelle," borne on the regimental colour and appointments, by royal authority, is commemorative of the gallantry of the second battalion of the Eighty-Seventh on this occasion.

During the remaining part of the year, the regiment was frequently engaged with the enemy in skirmishes.

Private Robert Smith, of the grenadiers, was, at the request of Sir

Charles Colville, promoted to be sergeant for his gallantry.

Volunteers Bourne and Bagenall, who were attached to the light company, were both severely wounded, and promoted to be ensigns for their gallant conduct. Sergeant Prideaux, of the light company, also distinguished himself.

In 1814 the army, strengthened by recruits and recovered men, continued its march into France, and on the 24th of February arrived at Salvatira.

The light company was engaged with those of the brigade, when a much superior force of the enemy attacked them; the light companies were in consequence recalled, and the brigade brought down to cover their retreat. On this occasion two rank and file were killed; Lieutenants Joseph Barry and William Wolsley Lanphier, with nine rank and file, wounded; and Lieutenant George Jackson taken prisoner.

On the 25th of February the regiment crossed the ford, attacked the French at Orthes on the 27th, and drove them from their entrenchments with immense loss. In this action the second battalion of the Eighty-Seventh regiment drew from the general officers in command the greatest praises for its bravery. It had one lieutenant, five sergeants, and eighty-seven rank and file killed; one major, four lieutenants, eight sergeants, and one hundred and fifty-eight rank and file wounded: total, two hundred and sixty-four. The strength in the field was five hundred and fifty-one.

Killed.
Lieutenant — James Fitz Gerald.
Wounded.
Major — Frederick Desbarres.
Lieutenant — William Mountgarrett.
      "   James Thompson,
      "   Grady,
      "   William Maginnis.

In commemoration of this battle, the Eighty-Seventh received the royal authority to bear the word "Orthes" on the regimental colour and appointments.

In an affair which took place on the 19th of March at Vic Bigorre, three rank and file were killed, and two lieutenants and twelve rank and file wounded: total, seventeen. The strength of the battalion was five hundred and seventy.

Having continued the pursuit of the enemy and crossed the River Garonne, four leagues below Toulouse, on the 5th of April, and attacked the French on the 10th of the same month at Toulouse on the left of the town, the redoubts were taken and retaken several times during the day. The enemy retreated at night, having suffered great loss; that of the Eighty-Seventh was one brevet major, four sergeants, one drummer, and twenty-two rank and file killed; one lieutenant, one ensign, six sergeants, and sixty-four rank and file wounded: total, one hundred. Its strength in the field was four hundred and sixty-four.

Patrick Connors never went into action without attracting the notice of his officers. On this occasion he particularly distinguished himself, and was promoted to the rank of sergeant, which situation he retained until his death.

Sergeant Carr, who was wounded at Tarifa, and served with credit in every action with the battalion, distinguished himself; likewise Sergeants Rideaux and Irwin. Lieutenant and Adjutant Moore had a horse shot under him. Private Thomas Byrne was also badly wounded, but recovered, and was promoted.

The royal authority was afterwards granted for the Eighty-Seventh to bear the word "Toulouse" on the regimental colour and appointments, in commemoration of the second battalion having shared in this battle.

During the night of the 11th of April the French troops evacuated Toulouse, and a white flag was hoisted. On the following day the Marquis of Wellington entered the city amidst the acclamations of the inhabitants. In the course of the afternoon of the 12th of April intelligence was received of the abdication of Napoleon; and had not the express been delayed on the journey by the French police, the sacrifice of many valuable lives would have been prevented.

A disbelief in the truth of this intelligence occasioned much unnecessary bloodshed at Bayonne, the garrison of which made a desperate sortie on the 14th of April, and Lieut.-General Sir John Hope (afterwards Earl of Hopetoun) was taken prisoner, Major-General Andrew Hay was killed, and Major-General Stopford was wounded. This was the last action of the Peninsular War.

A Treaty of Peace was established between Great Britain and France; Louis XVIII. was restored to the throne of his ancestors, and Napoleon Bonaparte was permitted to reside at Elba, the sovereignty of that island having been conceded to him by the allied powers. Prior to the breaking up of the Peninsular Army, the Duke of Wellington issued the following general order:

Bordeaux, 14th June 1814.

General Order.

The Commander of the Forces, being upon the point of returning to England, again takes this opportunity of congratulating the army upon the recent events which have restored peace to their country and to the world.

The share which the British Army have had in producing those events, and the high character with which the army will quit this country, must be equally satisfactory to every individual belonging to it, as they are to the Commander of the Forces, and he trusts that the troops will continue the same good conduct to the last.

The Commander of the Forces once more requests the army to accept his thanks.

Although circumstances may alter the relations in which he has stood towards them for some years so much to his satisfaction, he assures them he will never cease to feel the warmest interest in their welfare and honour, and that he will be at all times happy to be of any service to those to whose conduct, discipline, and gallantry their country is so much indebted.

In addition to the other distinctions acquired during the war in the Peninsula and the south of France, the Eighty-Seventh received the royal authority to bear the word "Peninsula" on the regimental colour and appointments.

The war being ended, the battalion marched from Toulouse to Blanch Fort, and embarked at Pouillac on the 7th of July, and arrived at Cork on the 20th of that month.

After being inspected, on landing at Cork, by the General commanding the district, the battalion was marched to Mallow to relieve the Twentieth regiment. It subsequently marched to the city of Limerick, and was stationed there for a few days, when orders were received for it to proceed to Middleton, in the county of Cork, to await the arrival of transports.

The battalion embarked at the Cove of Cork on the 23rd of August, and landed at Portsmouth, after a protracted voyage, on the 14th of September. On the day of disembarkation it proceeded *en route* to Horsham, where the depot of the regiment was stationed. After a stay of some days at Horsham, it marched to Plymouth for garrison duty, where it remained until December, having taken its tour of a month's duty over the American prisoners of war at Dartmoor.

On the 6th of December 1814 the battalion embarked for Guernsey, of which island General Sir John Doyle, Bart., the Colonel of the regiment, was Governor, and where it arrived on the 8th of that month.

The battalion continued on duty at Guernsey until the 2nd of April 1816, when it embarked for Portsmouth, from whence it marched to Colchester in September following.

On the 25th of January 1817, in pursuance of measures being taken for the reduction of the army, orders were received for the disbandment of the second battalion of the Eighty-Seventh regiment, on which occasion Lieut.-Colonel Sir Hugh Gough issued the following orders:—

Colchester Barracks, 24th January, 1817.
Regimental Orders.
It is with the most painful feeling of regret Lieut.-Colonel Sir Hugh Gough is necessitated to announce to the second battalion, Prince's Own Irish, that their services as a corps are no longer required, in consequence of the military arrangements it has been found necessary to adopt.

In making this distressing though necessary communication, and in taking leave of those brave officers and men, at whose head it has been Sir Hugh Gough's good fortune so long to have been placed, he feels himself on this occasion called upon to recapitulate the leading ones of so many brilliant achievements performed by his gallant comrades now about to separate. The recollection of such scenes must be a source of gratification to all, whether called on to serve their country in India, or to retire to their families and native land. To their command-

ing officer it ever has and ever will be, a source of heartfelt ex-
ultation. By their country and by their illustrious master, their
services have been duly appreciated, and nobly rewarded by
that designation, and by those badges so peculiar, so honourable, and so gratifying.

The Eighty-Seventh had the good fortune to serve under the
first general of the age, throughout the greater part of the Peninsular War, and longer than most corps in the service. At the
Battle of Talavera on the 27th of July, 1809 (when the battalion
first encountered the enemy), they had to sustain unsupported
the repeated attacks of the advance corps, and did not retire until both flanks were turned, the battalion nearly surrounded by
an infinitely superior force, and two-thirds of the officers and
men either killed or wounded. The movement of the regiment
to the rear, and its formation on the other corps of the division,
was a counterpart of their conduct, in having instantly recovered, on the first attack of the enemy, a temporary confusion
which was occasioned by the fire of a British regiment into the
rear of the battalion, the thickness of the wood having made it
impossible for that distinguished corps to have perceived the
new position which the Eighty-Seventh had taken up.

On this memorable occasion the charge of the two centre
companies did them and their officers the greatest honour. The
gallantry of the whole was conspicuous, and obtained the personal thanks of the brave officer who commanded the division, and who unfortunately fell on the following day, and also
the repeated thanks of the officer commanding the brigade.
(Major-General John Randoll McKenzie, who fell at Talavera
on the 28th of July 1809).

At the brilliant action of Barrosa the conduct of the Eighty-
Seventh in taking up the first position under a most destructive
fire from the enemy's artillery, and a column three times its
numbers, when it formed with the precision of parade movements, gave a happy omen of the issue of the day. The advance
of the battalion in line, its volley into the two battalions of the
eighth, and its charge on that corps, called for and received the
proudest meed of gallantry, the enthusiastic approbation of such
an officer as Sir Thomas Graham.

This charge was rewarded by the wreathed eagle of the Eighth
French regiment, and a howitzer: it led in a great measure to

the total discomfiture of the right column under General Laval, and nearly annihilated two battalions of one of the finest regiments in the French army: of one thousand six hundred men, which they brought into the field, only three hundred and fifty returned to Chiclana. The ready formation of the right wing from amidst the ranks of the retreating enemy, and their charge on the Fifty-Fourth French regiment, which at this moment attacked the right of the Eighty-Seventh, was rewarded by the marked approbation of their esteemed chief. The ultimate advance of the battalion on the enemy's guns was equally praiseworthy.

At Tarifa, a species of service new to the British Army called for a renewal of that steady gallantry which marked the conduct of the Eighty-Seventh at Barrosa. The immense superiority, in number, of the enemy, added enthusiasm to discipline: the cool intrepidity, the strict observance of orders, the exulting cheer when the enemy's columns pressed forward to the attack, proved the feelings which influenced the defenders of the breach of Tarifa, and was as honourable to them as soldiers, as their humane conduct to the wounded (when the enemy fled) was to their characters as men.

The persevering attention to their duty on the walls, in conjunction with their brave comrades, the second battalion of the Forty-Seventh, exposed to the continued fire of an enemy ten times the number of the garrison, and to the most dreadfully inclement weather, led to the ultimate abandonment of the siege, and was rewarded by the approbation of their general, their prince, and their country.

The Battle of Vittoria renewed the claim the Eighty-Seventh had to a place in the third division, and under its lamented leader, (Lieut.-General Sir Thomas Picton, G.C. B., who was killed at Waterloo on the 18th of June 1815), the battalion acquired fresh laurels. The charge of the Prince's Own on the hill crowned with the enemy's artillery, and covered with a strong column, called forth the marked approbation of Major-General the Honourable Charles Colville, as did the pursuit of that column, though flanked by a corps greatly superior in numbers. The cool steadiness with which they preserved their second position, under the fire and within a short range of a large portion of the enemy's field artillery, although the battalion at this time had lost upwards of half the number it took into the field, showed the steady perseverance in bravery and discipline which ever marked the glorious career of the corps.

The attack on the fortified hill at the action of the Nivelle, and the gallantry which rendered the conduct of the battalion so conspicuous in the subsequent attacks on that day, called for those animated expressions from Major-General the Honourable Charles Colville and Colonel John Keane, who commanded the division and brigade, 'Gallant Eighty-Seventh!' Noble 'Eighty-Seventh!' and deservedly were those titles bestowed. The actions of Orthes and Toulouse were also most glorious to the character of the corps, and its conduct was rewarded by the repeated thanks of the generals commanding.

Since the return of the Eighty-Seventh from service, they have shown, that to gallantry in the field, they add the most essential requisite in a soldier, orderly and correct conduct in garrison, which has acquired for them the approbation of every general officer under whom they have served, and the good wishes and esteem of the inhabitants with whom they have been placed.

While the foregoing detail will be most gratifying to the gallant men who have survived, the recital must also be consoling to the families of those who fell.

The Prince's Own Irish bled prodigally and nobly; they have sealed their duty to their king and country by the sacrifice of nearly two thousand of their comrades. But, while Lieut.-Colonel Sir Hugh Gough feels an honest pride in recounting these achievements, he wishes to caution his brother soldiers from assuming any exclusive right to pre-eminence over their gallant comrades; the Army of the Peninsula nobly did their duty, and repeatedly received the thanks of their Prince and their country.

In parting with the remains of that corps in which Sir Hugh Gough has served twenty-two years, at the head of which, and by whose valour and discipline, he has obtained those marks of distinction with which he has been honoured by his Royal Master, he cannot too emphatically express the most heartfelt acknowledgments and his deep regret.

From all classes of his officers he has uniformly experienced the most cordial and ready support. Their conduct in the field, while it called for the entire approbation of their commanding officer, acquired for them the best stay to military enterprise and military renown, *the confidence of their men*, and led to the accomplishment of their wishes, the Approbation of their Prince, the Honour of their Country, and the Character of their Corps. Every non-commissioned officer and man is equally entitled to the thanks of his commanding officer. To all he feels greatly indebted, and he begs to assure all, that their prosperity as individuals, or as a corps, will ever be the first wish of his heart, and to promote which he will consider no sacrifice or exertion too great.

The second battalion was disbanded at Colchester on the 1st of February 1817, having transferred to the first battalion three hundred and thirty effective men, most of whom were embarked in the same month, to join the first battalion in the Bengal Presidency.

LEONAUR

ALSO FROM LEONAUR
AVAILABLE IN SOFTCOVER OR HARDCOVER WITH DUST JACKET

ESCAPE FROM THE FRENCH *by Edward Boys*—A Young Royal Navy Midshipman's Adventures During the Napoleonic War.

THE VOYAGE OF H.M.S. PANDORA *by Edward Edwards R. N. & George Hamilton, edited by Basil Thomson*—In Pursuit of the Mutineers of the Bounty in the South Seas—1790-1791.

MEDUSA *by J. B. Henry Savigny and Alexander Correard and Charlotte-Adélaïde Dard* —Narrative of a Voyage to Senegal in 1816 & The Sufferings of the Picard Family After the Shipwreck of the Medusa.

THE SEA WAR OF 1812 VOLUME 1 *by A. T. Mahan*—A History of the Maritime Conflict.

THE SEA WAR OF 1812 VOLUME 2 *by A. T. Mahan*—A History of the Maritime Conflict.

WETHERELL OF H. M. S. HUSSAR *by John Wetherell*—The Recollections of an Ordinary Seaman of the Royal Navy During the Napoleonic Wars.

THE NAVAL BRIGADE IN NATAL *by C. R. N. Burne*—With the Guns of H. M. S. Terrible & H. M. S. Tartar during the Boer War 1899-1900.

THE VOYAGE OF H. M. S. BOUNTY *by William Bligh*—The True Story of an 18th Century Voyage of Exploration and Mutiny.

SHIPWRECK! *by William Gilly*—The Royal Navy's Disasters at Sea 1793-1849.

KING'S CUTTERS AND SMUGGLERS: 1700-1855 *by E. Keble Chatterton*—A unique period of maritime history-from the beginning of the eighteenth to the middle of the nineteenth century when British seamen risked all to smuggle valuable goods from wool to tea and spirits from and to the Continent.

CONFEDERATE BLOCKADE RUNNER *by John Wilkinson*—The Personal Recollections of an Officer of the Confederate Navy.

NAVAL BATTLES OF THE NAPOLEONIC WARS *by W. H. Fitchett*—Cape St. Vincent, the Nile, Cadiz, Copenhagen, Trafalgar & Others.

PRISONERS OF THE RED DESERT *by R. S. Gwatkin-Williams*—The Adventures of the Crew of the Tara During the First World War.

U-BOAT WAR 1914-1918 *by James B. Connolly/Karl von Schenk*—Two Contrasting Accounts from Both Sides of the Conflict at Sea During the Great War.

www.ingramcontent.com/pod-product-compliance
Lightning Source LLC
Chambersburg PA
CBHW021106090426
42738CB00006B/524